D1265460

MUSIC OF THE BIBLE

Da Capo Press Music Reprint Series

GENERAL EDITOR

FREDERICK FREEDMAN

VASSAR COLLEGE

THE

MUSIC OF THE BIBLE

WITH SOME ACCOUNT OF THE

DEVELOPMENT OF MODERN MUSICAL
INSTRUMENTS FROM ANCIENT TYPES

BY

JOHN STAINER

REVISED EDITION
WITH ADDITIONAL ILLUSTRATIONS AND SUPPLEMENTARY NOTES
BY FRANCIS W. GALPIN

𝄢 DA CAPO PRESS • NEW YORK • 1970

A Da Capo Press Reprint Edition

This Da Capo Press edition of John Stainer's *The Music of the Bible* is an unabridged republication of the revised edition published in London in 1914. It is reprinted by special arrangement with Novello and Company, Limited.

Library of Congress Catalog Card Number 74-100657

SBN 306-71862-6

Published by Da Capo Press
A Division of Plenum Publishing Corporation
227 West 17th Street, New York, N.Y. 10011

THE
MUSIC OF THE BIBLE

Frontispiece.

Sounding the Shophar. (p. 224.)

THE

MUSIC OF THE BIBLE

WITH SOME ACCOUNT OF THE

DEVELOPMENT OF MODERN MUSICAL INSTRUMENTS FROM ANCIENT TYPES

BY

JOHN STAINER

M.A., MUS. DOC., MAGD. COLL., OXON.

———————

NEW EDITION:

WITH ADDITIONAL ILLUSTRATIONS AND SUPPLEMENTARY NOTES
BY THE REV. F. W. GALPIN, M.A., F.L.S.

———————

LONDON: NOVELLO AND COMPANY, LIMITED.

———————

ORIGINAL PREFACE.

No apology is needed, I hope, for issuing in this form the substance of the series of articles which I contributed to the *Bible Educator*. Some of the statements which I brought forward in that work have received further confirmation by wider reading; but some others I have ventured to qualify or alter. Much new matter will be found here which I trust may be of interest to the general reader, if not of use to the professional.

I fully anticipate a criticism to the effect that such a subject as the development of musical instruments should rather have been allowed to stand alone than have been associated with Bible music. But I think all will admit that the study of the history of ancient nations, whether with reference to their arts, religion, conquests, or language, seems to gather and be concentrated round the Book of Books, and when once I began to treat of the comparative history of musical instruments, I felt that a few more words, tracing their growth up to our own times, would make this little work more complete and useful than if I should deal only with the sparse records of Hebrew music.

I have received, in all the philological portions of the book, much valuable help from my friend, ERNEST BUDGE (M.R.A.S.), of Christ's College, Cambridge; to whom also I am indebted for Appendixes II. and IV.

The transliteration of Hebrew words into our own tongue is always a difficult matter. I have uniformly spelt *kinnor* with a *k* instead of *c*, dreading lest readers should be tempted to pronounce it *sinnor*. The troublesome letter *ghain* has also been omitted from *ugab*. In other cases I hope the spelling will be found neither incorrect nor unpronounceable.

J. S.

EDITOR'S PREFACE.

WHEN, in the year 1879, *The Music of the Bible* was first issued in book form, our knowledge of the arts and habits of the bygone nations of the East, bordering on the Mediterranean Sea, was chiefly confined to the pioneer though splendid work of Botta and Layard in Assyria, and of Mariette and Wilkinson in Egypt ; but during the thirty and more years which have elapsed since then, new and unforeseen light has been thrown upon the conditions of life prevailing there in the far off centuries of the past. De Sarzec's and Peters's excavations in Babylonia, Flinders Petrie's magnificent discoveries in the tombs of Egypt, the graveyards of Goshen and the mounds of Philistia, Glaser's quest for Sabean inscriptions in Arabia, the explorations of the White Fathers at Carthage, and Wright's, Winckler's, Garstang's, and Hogarth's unveiling of the powers and resources of the Hittites, have placed students of Biblical archæology under fresh indebtedness to these and other toilers in the wide field of research. Nor is the tale yet complete ; for, at the dawn of this 20th century, Sir Arthur Evans, Dr. Halbherr,

and Miss Boyd have brought to light not only
on the Island of Crete, but in Egypt, Philistia,
Phœnicia, the coasts of Asia Minor, and prehistoric
Greece, the artistic marvels of Minoan civilization.

When considering, therefore, the extraneous
influences which affected the musical culture of
the Hebrews, we now have to reckon not merely
with the ancient monarchies of Assyria and Egypt,
but with those other gifted and great peoples with
whom in the course of their chequered history they
came in contact.

It has been said that the Jews were and are
a people without art; and certainly the poverty
of artistic treasure as yet discovered in Palestine
contrasts most unfavourably with the wealth of
those in countries surrounding. And although
there are antiquaries who still hope to find similar
relics in the Land of Promise, my own belief is
that such sculptured and painted scenes, for
instance, as have given us so vivid a picture of
Assyrian and Egyptian life, will never be forthcoming; and mainly for this reason, that the
Hebrews were bound by the laws of their race not
to make "any graven image or the likeness of
any thing that is in heaven above or in the earth
beneath or in the water under the earth," and
however they may have treated the other command-
ments, they obeyed this law so implicitly that
to-day we are without any illustrations of their
crafts or customs. Hence the great difficulty
experienced in obtaining any very definite
knowledge of the subject with which the present
work deals: for, dismissing delineations on coins
of late date as too crude in execution if not
fanciful in design, although we have the names

of the musical instruments which delighted this ancient people, except for the Roman sculpture of their sacred trumpets and Table of Shewbread on the Arch of victorious Titus, and the survival of the *shophar* of ram's horn at the present day— both ritual instruments, be it observed—we are not permitted to obtain even a glance of the forms they knew so well, as they accompanied the festive dance or swelled the sacred song.

Again, our knowledge of the evolution and distribution of musical instruments has greatly increased since the days when Carl Engel, from whose writings Sir John Stainer took much of his material, first drew prominent attention to the subject.

For these and other reasons a revised edition of *The Music of the Bible* appeared called for ; and although it would doubtless have been an easier task to produce an entirely new treatise than to amend and expand an existing text, yet the author's work was, as we should have expected, so conscientiously and attractively done that the way in which he presented the subject to the public has become, and still remains, popular, notwithstanding the fact that the book has been for many years out of print. The form, therefore, of the original publication has been retained, and my duty as editor has mainly consisted in rearranging obscure passages, correcting or omitting statements incompatible with more recent information, and adding to each chapter such Supplementary Notes as will place the reader in touch with the latest views and discoveries.

The old illustrations, moreover, have been kept, except in a few cases where they were either poorly executed or misleading, whilst others have been added where it was thought they would elucidate the text and notes.   As an interesting curiosity the author's classification of musical instruments in the Appendix has been reprinted, and one on more modern lines, and based on a systematic study of the various types, has been added for comparison.   There has also been given, in an additional Appendix (V.), a short account of the use of the *shophar* in the modern Synagogue.

For photographs of ancient sculpture and painting, as well as of actual instruments, I gratefully acknowledge my indebtedness to Professor Flinders Petrie, to Professor Garstang, to Professor Hogarth, Keeper of the Ashmolean Museum, Oxford, to the Rev. Père Delattre, Curator of the St. Louis Museum, Carthage, to the Director of the British Museum, to Messrs. Eyre & Spottiswoode, to Messrs. Holman (Philadelphia), and to Messrs. Suss of Whitechapel Road, E., for the excellent photograph of an Orthodox *shophar*-player, which by the kind assistance of a Jewish friend, has been taken especially for this work.

My thanks are also due to Mr. J. F. R. Stainer for permission to deal with his father's work in the way already indicated; and by so doing, I hope I may have rendered it in its new edition as great a source of pleasure and instruction to the rising generation of music-lovers as the original was to me in the now distant days of my youth.

FRANCIS W. GALPIN.

Hatfield Vicarage, Harlow.

March, 1914.

CONTENTS.

INTRODUCTION.

PAGE

Origin of Singing and Musical Instruments. Probable
Sources of Ancient Hebrew Music. Modern
Hebrew Music. Works of Reference 1

PART I. (STRINGED INSTRUMENTS).

CHAPTER I.—The Kinnor: formerly thought to have
been a Trigon. Illustrations of Trigons. Now
believed to have been a Lyre. Ancient Lyres.
Difference between Lyre and Guitar 13

CHAPTER II.—The Nebel: probably a moderate-sized
Harp. Position of Harp when held by Player.
Long-necked Instruments of the Egyptians: their
importance. Frets. Ancient Harps. Link
between Harp and Guitar. The Nebel-azor ... 28

CHAPTER III.—Sabeca, probably a Harp. Psanterin.
Antiquity of Psalteries and Dulcimers. The
History of the word Psanterin. The develop-
ment of the Dulcimer into the modern Pianoforte 48

CHAPTER IV.—Kithros, the Greek Lyre. Explanation
of several Words used in the headings and
elsewhere in the Psalms. The intimate relation
between all Stringed Instruments 69

PART II. (WIND INSTRUMENTS).   PAGE

CHAPTER V.—Khalil : probably an Oboe. Distinction between various Reed Pipes. Derivation of various names given to Flutes. Flûtes à bec. Flauto traverso. Ancient Flutes. Modern Egyptian Reed Instruments. The Double Pipe. Machol. Mahalath   95

CHAPTER VI.—Ugab. Ancient Syrinx. Magrepha. The Organ: suggested process of evolution. First principles of its construction. Chinese Organ. Hydraulic Organ. Mashrokitha   115

CHAPTER VII.—Sumponyah: account of the name. Ancient Bagpipes   145

CHAPTER VIII. — Keren, Shophar, Khatsotsrah : difference between them. Ancient Horns. Ancient Trumpets   153

PART III. (INSTRUMENTS OF PERCUSSION).

CHAPTER IX.—Tseltslim, Mtsiltayim. Ancient Cymbals. Arabian Cymbals. Little Cymbals. Metzilloth. Connection between Cymbals and Bells. Pha-amon   166

CHAPTER X.—Menaaneim. Ancient Sistra or Rattles. Shalishim. Toph: a Tambour. Ancient Tambours   178

PART IV. (VOCAL MUSIC).

CHAPTER XI.—Signs directing ascent or descent of the Voice in reciting Poetry or Sacred Books. Accents. Greek Church Musical Notation. Hebrew Accents. Neumes. Ancient Scales. Ancient Melodies. Chants   192

APPENDICES.

I.—Two general Classifications of Musical Instruments   216

II.—Hebrew, Greek, and Latin Names of Bible Instruments   218

III.—Principal Passages in the Bible in which Musical Instruments are mentioned   219

IV.—List of Hebrew Accents   222

V.—The Shophar in the Synagogue   224

INDEX   227

LIST OF PLATES.

Frontispiece :—SOUNDING THE SHOPHAR.

PAGE

PLATE   I.   (A.) THE LYRE   14
A bas-relief found at Tell-Loh, the site of the
Palace of Gudea, an early Babylonish King
(3000-2800 B.C.).

(B.) THE LONG-NECKED LUTE OR GUITAR
Early Babylonish sculpture (*c.* 2500 B.C.).

PLATE   II.   THE LYRE   20
From a sarcophagus discovered at Aghia
Triada, Crete—Minoan Art (*c.* 1400 B.C.).

PLATE   III.   THE LONG-NECKED LUTE OR GUITAR...   26
From a sculptured slab found in the ruins of
the Hittite Palace at Eyuk, near Sinope, in
Asia Minor (*c.* 1000 B.C.).

PLATE   IV.   THE SHORT-NECKED LUTE 26*a*
Pottery figure discovered in a Goshen
cemetery (Saft - el - Henna). Probably
Minoan or early Greek Art (*c.* 1200 B.C.).

PLATE   V.   THE TRIANGULAR HARP   44
An Egyptian Statuette in Wood, probably
from Thebes (*c.* 1300 B.C.).

PLATE   VI.   THE BOW-SHAPED HARP...   46
The modern Burmese *Soung*, almost identical
with the ancient Egyptian Harp.

PLATE   VII.   THE WATER-ORGAN *(Hydraulus)*   ...   140
Pottery model discovered in the ruins of
Carthage. Græco-Roman Art (*c.* 120 A.D.).

PAGE

PLATE VIII. THE WATER-ORGAN (GALPIN COLLEC-
             TION) 140*a*
             Showing the front view of the working
             reproduction.

PLATE   IX. THE WATER-ORGAN (GALPIN COLLEC-
             TION) 140*b*
             Showing the back view and Key-board.

PLATE   X. THE SACRED TRUMPETS *(Khatsotsrah)* ...   160
             Depicted, together with the Table of Shew-
             bread and the "Golden Candlestick," on
             the Arch of Titus. Rome (*c.* 80 A.D.).

PLATE   XI. CORNETTS AND SACKBUT (GALPIN COLLEC-
             TION)   164
             1. High Treble Cornett, 1518.   2. Treble
             Cornett, 17th cent.   3. Mute Cornett,
             17th cent.   4. Sackbut by Neuschel of
             Nuremberg, 1557.

MUSIC OF THE BIBLE.

INTRODUCTION.

No art is exercising such a strong influence over
the human race at the present time as the art of
Music. It has become so thoroughly a part of our
existence that we rarely pause to consider to what
an extent we are, as it were, enveloped in its sweet
sounds, or how irremediable its loss would be to us.
As a natural result of this, much interest has of
late years been shown in every research which
might tend to throw some light on its early history.
The various musical instruments depicted in
sculpture, or on coins, or sometimes luckily found
in ancient tombs, have been carefully examined,
with excellent results. Also, the broad basis on
which the study of History now stands has allowed
opportunities of comparing the music and musical
instruments of ancient nations, and of classifying
them into different families. It will at once be
seen what important results must arise from this,
for in company with customs, words, and even
modes of thought, musical instruments may pass
from one nation to another, whether their intercourse has been that of peaceful neighbours or of
tyrannic foes.

But notwithstanding all that has been done towards elucidating the mysteries of the birth of Music, no precise data can be obtained on this point. The stories common among the ancient Greeks about the discovery of the lyre by Mercury, formed of strings stretched across a tortoise-shell (*testudo*)* ; of Orpheus, and his transmitting his knowledge of music to Thamyris and Linus; of Terpander, and his improvements in the art—are all very pretty, and sometimes also not a little amusing, when it is found that learned men find in them ample grounds for serious discussion; but as a matter of fact, nothing is known as to the origin of music. Nor is it a subject for regret that so lovely, so ethereal an art should hide its head in obscurity. It has come down to our time in rich profusion, like some noble stream, and all that we can discover, if we attempt to retrace its course, is that on all sides and at all times welling springs have found their way into its bosom, each of which has its claim to our gratitude as administering to our plenty, but of no one of which can we say, this is the fountain-head of our art. The origin of music is inseparable from the origin of language, and whatever views are held with regard to the one, will hold good of the other. But without entering into any digression on this subject, it may be said

---

* According to the Hymn to Hermes (at one time attributed to Homer), the god, "soon after his birth, found a mountain tortoise grazing near his grotto, on Mount Kyllene. He disembowelled it, took its shell, and, out of the back of the shell he formed the lyre. He cut two stalks of reed of equal length, and, boring the shell, he employed them as arms or sides (πήχεις) to the lyre. He stretched the skin of an ox over the shell. It was, perhaps, the inner skin, to cover the open part, and thus to give it a sort of leather or parchment front. Then he tied cross-bars of reed to the arms, and attached seven strings of sheep-gut to the cross-bars. After that, he tried the strings with a plectrum."—*Chappell's* "*History of Music,*" p. 29.

that *singing* is really little else than a highly
beautiful *speaking*   A French writer* says—" A
very important characteristic of ancient languages
was rhythm.   The more or less regular recurrence
of intonations and of similar cadences constitutes
for children and savages the most agreeable form
of music.   The more the rhythm is accentuated,
the better they are pleased ; they love not only its
sound, but its movement also. . . . The most
civilised nations cannot escape from this tyranny of
rhythm. . . . Rhythm seems, indeed, to contain
some general law, possessing power over almost
all living things.   One might say that rhythm is
the dance of sound, as dancing is the rhythm of
movement.   The further we go back into the past,
the more marked and dominant is it found in
language.   It is certain that at one period of the
development of humanity, rhythm constituted the
only music known, and that it was even intertwined
with language itself."   It is true that in singing
the voice is modulated and regulated by rules, the
practice of which has now become a complicated
art; but, on the other hand, is there not music,
and that of the most touching kind, on many a
speaker's lips—on those of the earnest preacher,
the anxious mother, the loving friend ?   And this
is not the less *music* because it has not been
successfully analysed, or because its laws are not
published cheaply in a tabulated form.   May we
not say, then, that vocal music would naturally
grow out of sweet talk, and may we not
give to vocal music priority of existence over
instrumental ?   But, alas ! the early history
of the human race discloses more of common

* Eugène Véron on Æsthetics.   Translated by Armstrong.

strife and bloodshed than of peace, and from the
natural and indissoluble link between music and
rhythm we soon find music, especially as practised
on instruments of percussion, an ingredient of war.
It would answer two purposes : instruments of
brilliant tone, such as trumpets and horns, would
excite and rouse the feelings, while drums and
rattles would enforce the rhythmical stepping and
close movement of large bodies of men.   And,
again, the known effect of music upon the emotions
would soon enlist it to the cause of religion ; and
music, therefore, seems amongst all nations to have
been as much a part of worship as of war.

The division of the Music of the Bible into
three kinds—namely, as used in worship, war, and
social intercourse—naturally suggests itself; and
it would be an exceedingly good division, if only
there existed sufficient materials for its story.
But unfortunately direct information on the
subject is most scanty ; for often that which seems
at first sight a plain statement of facts, will on
examination turn out far otherwise.   For instance,
we are told that Jubal was " the father of such as
handle the harp and the organ."   This reads thus
in the Lutheran version : " Und sein Bruder hiesz
Jubal, von dem sind hergekommen die Geiger und
Pfeifer " (" And his brother was named Jubal, from
whom descended *fiddlers* and *pipers* ").   On turning
to the Septuagint version, we shall find that no less
than three totally distinct words are used in
different parts of the Bible to translate the word
we render " organ."*   We must therefore look to
the nations with which the Jews came into contact

---

* ψαλτήριον, Gen. iv. 21 ; ψαλμός, Job. xxi. 12 and xxx. 31 ; ὄργανον,
Ps. cl. 4.

as the best source of information. We shall soon
in this manner find valuable matter. For instance,
Laban is said to have regretted the suddenness of
Jacob's departure, because it deprived him of the
opportunity of sending him away with music.
"Wherefore didst thou flee away secretly, and
steal away from me; and didst not tell me, that
I might have sent thee away with mirth, and with
songs, with tabret, and with harp?" (Gen. xxxi.
27). *Kinnor*, or *cinnor*, is the word here used for
"harp," and it is the only stringed instrument
mentioned in the Pentateuch. Laban being a
Syrian, we shall be justified in believing this to be
a Syrian instrument, and not, as sometimes stated,
of Phœnician origin. This text also shows that
music was used for home festivals. But it must
not be expected that, as an art, music could reach
a very high standard amongst nomadic tribes
whose roof was never more substantial than
a tent, whose temple of worship was the canopy
of heaven.

The intercourse between Abraham and the
Canaanites in all probability influenced future
Hebrew music. Then follows Jacob's residence
with Laban, alluded to above, which probably
caused his posterity to carry a certain amount of
Syriac music, or musical instruments, into Egypt.
But, again, a stay of four centuries in so civilised a
country as Egypt must have largely added to their
knowledge of the art; and it seems not unfair to
suppose that whatever system of notation the
Hebrews adopted was learned from the Egyptians.
The strong love of poetry amongst the Jews is
shown by frequent allusions in Holy Scripture
even as early as the Pentateuch; but where did

they learn to set their inspired songs to tunes? In all probability in Egypt; and, unpleasant as it may sound to say so, the glorious song of Moses was most probably sung to some simple Egyptian chant, well known and popular. It may be said, "Why ascribe all the *invention* of the art to the neighbours of the Jews, and deny to the Jews the power of forming their own melodies and their own instruments?" The reply is simple—pastoral duties and a pastoral mode of life, as a matter of fact, do not tend to foster constructive art in such a manner as the concentration of highly-educated men in large cities; and whereas the Jews, during their stay in Egypt, could have had but small opportunities of inventing or elaborating a system of music, the Egyptians themselves had the most favourable opportunities not only then, but for centuries previous to the immigration of the Hebrews. Their learning was notorious, and it is an accepted fact that music was a recognised branch of their learning. But, to continue: the wandering in the wilderness could not conduce to artistic progress, nor did more favourable opportunities present themselves after the establishment of the Jews in the promised land under Joshua, for they then passed through some five centuries of almost constant warfare with neighbouring nations. And it must not be forgotten that Solomon had to employ foreign workmen for all delicate work, and probably, therefore, for the construction of musical instruments. We read, "And the king made of the almug trees pillars for the house of the Lord, and for the king's house, *harps also and psalteries for singers:* there came no such almug trees, nor were seen unto this day" (1 Kings x. 12). Then, again, after the time of Solomon the troubled state of divided Israel was most unsuited to the cultivation of native art, while on the other hand the constant intercourse of the Jews with the Assyrians, and their forced residence among them while in captivity, must have modified existing music or have given it some fresh ingredients.

It may be said, therefore, on the whole, that the internal condition of the Jews offered at any time but a poor nursery for art, but that their external relations rendered an incorporation of the arts of their neighbours inevitable. It is, of course, possible to push this argument too far, and to deny that the Jews possessed any national music. This would be wrong, because it is more than probable that whatever they adopted from their neighbours would be moulded by them into a shape most pleasing to them, and in time would assume peculiarities of style which would distinguish it from its parent stock.

It might be supposed that much assistance in treating of the music of the Bible might be obtained from an examination of the music now in use in the synagogues of the Jews. But the most that could be discovered from such a source would be partial traditions of the music of the *second* Temple; and undoubtedly the music of the second Temple not only fell far short of that of the first in point of efficiency and number of executants, but was also tinctured with the foreign associations of the returning Jews. Such instruments as had been lately adopted would most likely be used on the restoration of their worship, and it is not improbable that the vocal music also would be modified. Some of those instruments might have been

introduced, the Chaldean names of which appear
in the book of Daniel. But this is not all: a
comparison of the music used in modern synagogues
shows that even since the dispersion of the nation
their art has been influenced by that of the people
amongst whom they have settled. An important
fact bearing on this is noticed by Carl Engel (in his
valuable work on National Music), namely, that
"in the synagogal hymns of the Sephardic Jews
who were expelled from the Spanish Peninsula at
the end of the fifteenth century, distinct traces of
the characteristics of Moorish music are still
preserved." The following important passage
bearing on this subject is from the pen of the
Rev. D. A. de Sola :* "When the Sephardic ritual
became fixed and generally established in Spain,
and was enriched by the solemn hymns of Gabirol,
Judah Ha-levi, and other celebrated Hebrew
poets, chants or melodies were composed or
adapted to them, and were soon generally adopted.
It would, indeed, have been most desirable that
the sublime lays of our pious poets should have
ever been found combined with equally sublime
and sweet strains by devotionally inspired musical
composers of our own nation. But this was not
always practicable; and at a very early period it
became necessary to sing many of these hymns to
the popular melodies of the day; and in most
printed editions we find directions prefixed to
hymns, replete with piety and devotion, that
they are to be sung to the tune of ' *Permetid,
bella Amaryllis* ' (' Permit, fair Amaryllis '),

---

* See p. 13 of this author's learned preface to the *Ancient Melodies of the
Liturgy of the Spanish and Portuguese Jews*. (London, 1857.) Also
supplementary notes to Chapter XI. *infra*.

'*Tres colores in una*' ('Three colours in one'),
'*Temprano naçes, Almendro*' ('Thou buddest soon,
O Almond'), and similar ancient Spanish or
Moorish songs — a practice no doubt very
objectionable, for obvious reasons, and from which
the better taste of the present age would shrink. It
is, however, but fair to say that these adaptations,
though in some degree unavoidable, did not pass
without severe censure from pious and learned
rabbis." Similarly, it will be found that in every
case the modern music of the Jews varies remark-
ably according to the music of nations in which
they have formed colonies, whether those colonies
be in Germany, Holland, France, or Portugal.
It is however noticeable that in many of the most
carefully preserved melodies there is a decided
cast of Asiatic tonality. If the traditions of the
second Temple exist anywhere in a tolerably pure
state, they may perhaps be discovered amongst the
descendants of those Jews who migrated to Egypt
about 200 years before Christ, to avoid the tyranny
of the Seleucides, and who built a temple near
Heliopolis.

That there should be a sad lack of national
monuments relating to the Jews is not surprising,
when it is remembered that Jerusalem stood about
seventeen sieges, each of which was accompanied
by more or less destruction, and that, too, at the
hands of victors who seemed to take a malicious
delight in effacing the national characteristics of
those they conquered. So successful have they
been that there remains not one *Jewish* bas-relief
to tell the shape of their musical instruments, and
only on a few coins of late date drawings of
instruments, of a not very intelligible character,

are known to exist. This being the case, the reader will sometimes have to content himself with the opinions, often contradictory, of learned men. *

But we ought, nevertheless, not to undervalue the study of what may perhaps be appropriately termed the comparative anatomy of musical instruments. For it is easy to discern in the records of history that such instruments have been undesignedly moulded into very clearly defined groups or classes, according to the uses for which they were intended, these uses varying, of course, with the national tastes and occupations of the races by whom they were adopted. Strong probability, sometimes almost approaching to certainty, may therefore be thus established as to the nature of a musical instrument, the actual description of which may be of the most scanty kind, the arguments pursued being on much the same method as that familiar to naturalists, who are not uncommonly able to give a fairly trustworthy account of the form and physiological construction of some bird or beast, of which only a few bones remain, dug out of some early stratum of the earth's surface. And as even the habits of such extinct animals can often be gathered from a careful study of their natural environment, so, too, may the character and capabilities of a musical instrument be discovered by considering the occasions on which it is recorded to have been used.

We propose now to give a short account of every instrument mentioned in Holy Scripture, stating what is known as to its construction, origin, and uses. For this purpose we will divide them, as a

* See also Editor's Preface.

modern orchestra would be divided, into string instruments, wind instruments, and instruments of percussion; pointing out the relation they bear to kindred instruments of our own time. If this account of Hebrew instruments be followed by a notice of Hebrew vocal music, it is hoped that the reader will have gained some useful knowledge of the music of the Bible.

The following General Treatises of Recent
Date may be Consulted :—

On Hebrew Music.

Riehm, E. C. A.   Handwörterbuch des biblischen
Altertums (Bielefeld, 1893).

Weiss, J.   Die musikalischen Instrumente in den heiligen
Schriften des Alten Testamentes (Graz, 1895).

Wellhausen, J.   The Book of Psalms (with an Appendix
on Music), (London, 1898).

Cheyne and Black.   Encyclopædia Biblica (*s.v.* Music,
Psalms), (London, 1902).

Hastings, J.   Dictionary of the Bible (*s.v.* Music, &c.),
(Edinburgh, 1909).

Schaff and Herzog.   Encyclopædia of Religious
Knowledge (*s.v.* Music), (New York 1905-12).

On Archæological Research.

Ball, C. J.   Light from the East (London, 1899).

Hilprecht, H. V.   Explorations in Bible Lands
(Philadelphia, 1903).

Moore, M.   Carthage of the Phœnicians (London, 1905).

Mosso, A.   The Dawn of Mediterranean Civilisation
(London, Leipsic, 1910).

Garstang, J.   The Land of the Hittites (London, 1910).

On the Evolution of Musical Instruments.

Smith, Hermann.   The World's Earliest Music (London,
1904).

Schlesinger, K.   Precursors of the Violin Family (London,
1910).

Galpin, F. W.   Old English Instruments of Music
(London, 1911).

Encyclopædia Britannica (*s.v.* Musical Instruments),
11th Ed. (Cambridge, 1911).

References to important papers and pamphlets will be
found in the Supplementary Notes to each chapter.

PART I.

STRINGED INSTRUMENTS.

CHAPTER I.

THE KINNOR.

THE first instrument mentioned in the Bible is the *kinnor*, translated " harp " in our version. Jubal was " the father of such as handle the *kinnor* and *ugab* " (Gen. iv. 21). Authorities are divided as to whether the *kinnor* was a harp or a lyre. There have been attempts to show that it was a *trigon*, or three-cornered harp, specimens of which are depicted on some Egyptian bas-reliefs, and which must have been known to the Romans and Greeks. Nicomachus mentions the *trigon* as having been adjusted by Pythagoras after discovering the ratios of consonant harmonics. The simplest forms of the *trigon** would be as shown in Figs. 1, 2, and 3 ; and it is probable that one of the characteristics of the instrument was that there existed only two sides of wooden frame, the third side being formed by the longest string, as shown in the following illustrations (Figs. 4, 5, and 6), which are copied from tombs at Thebes and Dekkeh.

* As given by Blanchinus, "De tribus generibus instrumentorum musicæ veterum organicæ Dissertatio." (Romæ, 1742.)

It will be observed that the instrument was not placed upon the ground, but was held under the arm, or was rested upon the shoulder (*see* Fig. 7).* The termination of one of the sides with the head of a

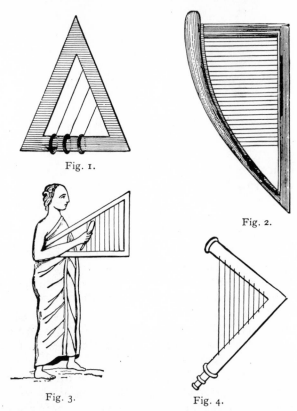

Fig. 1.

Fig. 2.

Fig. 3.

Fig. 4.

bird (probably a goose) would be forbidden among the Jews, who might not make an image of any animal or beast. The next illustration (Fig. 8)

* Taken from a Pompeian fresco, a copy of which was in the author's possession.

(A.)

(B.)

I. (A.) THE LYRE.—BABYLONIAN ART: *c.* 3000 B.C. (p. 26.)
    (B.) THE LONG-NECKED LUTE OR GUITAR.—BABYLONIAN ART·
       c. 2500 B.C. (p. 46.)

shows a very curious instrument in the museum at Florence.

Some authors assert that the *kinnor* had nine strings, others ten. The instrument had, according

Fig. 5.   Fig. 6.

Fig. 7.   Fig. 8.

to Fétis,* nine strings of camel-gut, but according to Dr. Jebb,† only eight strings. The latter author grounds his decision on the fact that the

* *Histoire Générale de la Musique*, vol. i., p. 384.
† *A Literal Translation of the Psalms.* (Longmans.) Dissertation ii.

kinnor is associated with the word *sheminith* (*see* 1 Chron. xv. 21), just as *alamoth* is with *nebel*, and that *sheminith* is undoubtedly connected with the number 8, being rendered in the Septuagint ὑπὲρ τῆς ὀγδοής, " on the eighth." * Dr. Jebb thinks Josephus† right in saying that the *kinnor* was played by a *plectrum* (πλῆκτρον) or small staff of quill, bone, or ivory, which the ancients often used

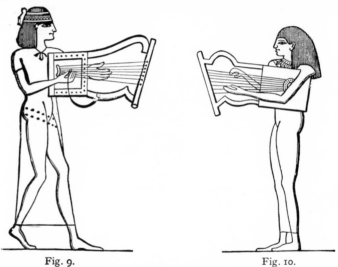

Fig. 9.   Fig. 10.

instead of the tips of their fingers; but Josephus is probably wrong in saying that the *kinnor* had ten strings and the *nebel* twelve, for the *kinnor* had not more than eight or nine strings. But David apparently used no plectrum—that is, if the words, " David took an harp (*kinnor*), and played with his

---

* See, however, Supplementary Note (2) to Chapter IV.

† ἡ μὲν κινύρα δέκα χορδαῖς ἐξημμένη τύπτεται πλήκτρῳ· ἡ δὲ νάβλα δώδεκα φθόγγους ἔχουσα τοῖς δακτύλοις κρούεται.

hand" (1 Sam. xvi. 23), are to be understood as implying that he used nothing but his hand, a somewhat forced interpretation.

But natural as was the hypothesis that the *kinnor* was a simple harp, to those who specially directed their attention to the instruments of the early European nations, further knowledge of Egyptian and Assyrian antiquities led to the suggestion (by Pfeiffer, Winer, and other authors)

Fig. 11.

that the *kinnor* was, after all, a sort of *guitar*. This idea was combated by Dr. Kitto, who brought forward many sound reasons for believing that it was a *lyre*.* If this idea be correct, the *kinnor* may have been very similar in form, perhaps even identical with, the instruments shown in Figs. 9, 10, 11.

* See Supplementary Note 1, to this Chapter.

It was sometimes played in an upright position, as shown in the illustration (Fig. 11). The arguments in favour of the *kinnor* being a lyre are based upon certain other representations, the most important of which was discovered by Sir Gardner Wilkinson* in a tomb at Beni Hassan. It is a painting representing the arrival of a company of strangers in Egypt. The discoverer suggests that these strangers are no less than Joseph's brethren. He describes them thus: "The first figure is an

Fig. 12.

Egyptian scribe, who presents an account of their arrival to a person seated, the owner of the tomb, and one of the principal officers of the reigning Pharaoh. The next, also an Egyptian, ushers them into his presence; and two advance, bringing presents—the wild goat or ibex, and the gazelle, the productions of their country. Four men, carrying bows and clubs, follow, leading an ass, on which two children are placed in panniers,

* *Manners and Customs of the Ancient Egyptians*, vol. ii., p. 296.

accompanied by a boy and four women; and, last of all, another ass laden, and two men (Fig. 12)— one holding a bow and club, the other a lyre, which he plays with the plectrum. . . . The

Fig. 13.

lyre is rude, and differs a little in form from those generally used in Egypt."

The authenticity of this unique picture, as representing the arrival of the sons of Jacob, would

set the question of the shape of the *kinnor* at rest
for ever; but, unfortunately, it remains only a
probability.   At any rate, the figures portrayed
are plainly Semitic.

The other representation which has been brought
forward as testifying to the shape of the *kinnor* is

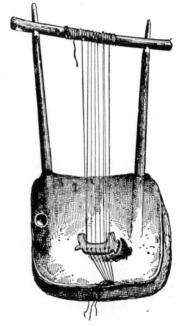

Fig. 14.

a bas-relief in the British Museum, on which is
shown an Assyrian in charge of captives who are
playing on lyres (Fig. 13).   If Layard is right in
supposing these to be *Jewish* captives, it is certain
that the *kinnor* was a lyre, because it was their
kinnors which they mournfully hung up in the trees

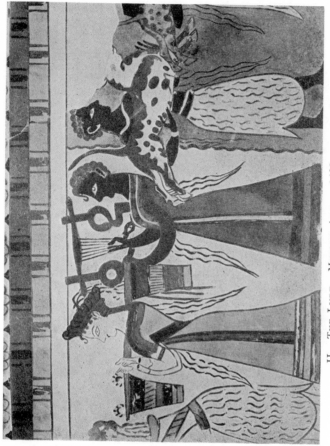

II. The Lyre.—Minoan Art: c. 1400 b.c. (p. 26.)

overhanging the "rivers of Babylon." "We hanged
our *kinnors* upon the willows in the midst thereof "
(Ps. cxxxvii. 2).

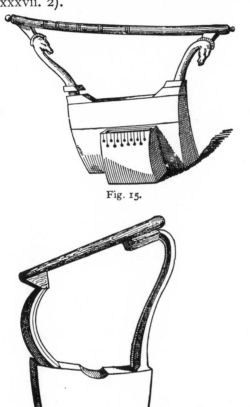

Fig. 15.

Fig. 16.

But M. Fétis gives very good reasons for believing
that these captives are not Jews, but Barabras or

Berbers, for they are, he says, performing on the *kissar*, or Ethiopian lyre, which is depicted in Fig. 14. This illustration shows one of the specimens given by the Viceroy of Egypt to the Victoria and Albert Museum, South Kensington. It has strings of camel-gut (as had also the *kinnor*), and a plectrum made of horn is used by itself, or with the fingers, or alternately, by the player. Engel says that the *kissar* is certainly one of the most ancient stringed instruments known.

Considering the great likeness between the outline of the *kissar* and the *kinnor* in some of the illustrations, it is not surprising that some authors have treated them as identical. There is, however, one reason why the lyres represented in Fig. 13 should not be *Jewish* instruments—namely, the outer part of the framework is terminated at each end with the head of a bird or snake, which, as has been before remarked, would not be found on their *kinnors*.

Two very elegant Egyptian lyres are depicted in Figs. 15 and 16—one from the Leyden collection, the other from that at Berlin.

The *kinnor* was made of wood—David made it of *berosh*, but it is recorded that Solomon made some of *almug* wood for use in the Temple (1 Kings x. 12). Whatever be the exact wood signified by *almug*, the value of it was evidently very great.* The *kinnor* was one of the instruments mentioned by Laban the Syrian, as before noticed, a fact which goes far to prove its Syrian origin, although it seems to have been considered

---

* Josephus speaks of *kinnors* made of *electrum* (ἤλεκτρον), a mixed metal, not *amber*—a meaning this word also had. Probably the pegs only or other small details were made of this material. See note, p. 38.

Phœnician by some of the ancients. The name is
traced to a Syrian root—*kinroth*. The instrument
was used on joyous occasions—on the bringing
back of the ark (1 Chron. xvi. 4–6), the account of
which shows the importance attached to proficiency
on the part of the performers : " And he appointed
certain of the Levites to minister before the ark of
the Lord, and to record, and to thank . . . the

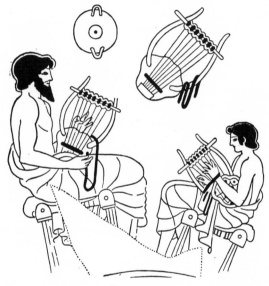

Fig. 17.

Lord God of Israel . . . Jeiel with psalteries and
with *kinnors;* but Asaph made a sound with cymbals;
Benaiah also and Jahaziel the priests with trumpets
continually before the ark of the covenant of God."
Again, in 1 Chron. xxv. 3, the *kinnor* was ordered
to be used by high and important families, as an
accompaniment to their prophecy. The sons of

Jeduthun are mentioned as prophesying with a *kinnor*. It was also carried by wandering female minstrels—the "Bayadères" of to-day—whose character was bad, if one may judge from the allusion to them in Isa. xxiii. 16, where the prophet utters thoughts of indignant irony against Tyre: "Take a *kinnor*, go about the city, thou harlot that hast been forgotten; make sweet melody, sing many songs, that thou mayest be remembered." The people under Jehoshaphat, returning with joy to Jerusalem after overcoming the Moabites, made joyful sounds "with psalteries and *kinnors* and trumpets" (2 Chron. xx. 28). The carrying of the *kinnor* by the captives in Babylon has before been alluded to. It was also the instrument which, touched by the hand of the youthful and God-beloved David, drove away the wicked spirit of Saul: "And it came to pass, when the evil spirit from God was upon Saul, that David took a *kinnor*, and played with his hand: so Saul was refreshed, and was well, and the evil spirit departed from him" (1 Sam. xvi. 23).

The reader will by this time have balanced the probabilities as to the nature and construction of the *kinnor;* and most likely he will conclude that it was either a guitar or more probably a lyre, a belief which seems to be gaining ground, on account of the aptitude of such instruments for the uses to which the *kinnor* was devoted.

As there is often much confusion amongst non-musicians as to the real distinction between a lyre and a lute (or a guitar) two illustrations are given, one (Fig. 17) showing a Greek music-master teaching a youth to play on the lyre, the other (Fig. 18) showing a man playing on a lute. From these

illustrations it will be distinctly understood that
there is nothing behind the upper portion of the
strings of a lyre ; while, on the contrary, the strings
of guitars and lutes are carried upwards beyond the
body or *resonance-box*, over a piece of wood called
the *neck*, on which is fastened the smooth piece
of wood called the *finger-board*, because on to
its surface the fingers press the strings when
playing.* It will be observed that a guitar and

Fig. 18.

lute only vary with regard to the shape or length
of the body and neck ; both instruments are of one
family.

SUPPLEMENTARY NOTES.

(1.) The reasons for supposing that the Hebrew *Kinnor*
was identical with the lyre are very strong. In the first
place, the lyre is the earliest practical form of stringed

* See Supplementary Note (2), to this Chapter.

instrument of which we have any representation, for it is figured on a fragment of a bas-relief found at Tell-Loh, among the ruins of the palace of an early Babylonish king, Gudea (3000-2800 B.C.), where it not only appears with eleven strings but in a shape which suggests that it was already an elaboration of a yet earlier and simpler instrument (Plate IA.). In the same way the *kinnor* appears in Bible history as the first and representative type of all stringed instruments. Secondly, it was always considered the national instrument of the Hebrews—the favourite of David, their greatest king and hero: for this reason the lyre—in some of its later forms—appears on Jewish coins (Figs. 43, 44, 45) as, towards the close of the Middle Ages, the Irish Harp was stamped on those of Ireland. Thirdly, the ancient Egyptian name for the lyre seems to have been *Kn-an-aul*, which is closely akin to the word *kinnor*. And lastly, in early Arabic versions of the Scriptures the Hebrew *kinnor* is frequently translated *kissari*, a transliteration of the word *kithara*, still surviving in the name of the Ethiopian lyre (Fig. 14).

As a generic name the word *kinnor* no doubt included both the primitive and the more elaborate forms of the instrument, for in Egypt more than three thousand years ago lyres were made of considerable size and power, some having from ten to eighteen strings, though it does not seem to have been so peculiarly associated with the religious ceremonies of that country as the bow-shaped harp (Figs. 23, 24, 26). Probably it was an importation from Western Asia. By the year 1400 B.C. it appears in the Minoan civilisation of Crete, for on a sarcophagus discovered at Aghia Triada it is figured in the hands of a Cretan performer with seven strings and an artistically shaped frame, whilst another man plays the double reed-pipe (Plate II.).

(2.) The difference between the lyre-form and the guitar-form is really greater than the author allows. Although Miss K. Schlesinger (*Precursors of the Violin Family*) has tried to show that the European guitar shape, with flexuous sides, was evolved from the *kithara* or later lyre-form, basing her conclusions upon a series of

III. THE LONG-NECKED LUTE OR GUITAR.—HITTITE ART:
c. 1000 B.C. (pp. 27, 94, 152.)

IV. The Short-Necked Lute.—Minoan Art: c. 1200 B.C. (p. 27.)

drawings appended, probably by an Alexandrine artist
(*c.* 600 A.D.), to an illuminated MS. of the *Utrecht
Psalter*, it is quite evident from discoveries in Western
Asia that the typical forms of lyre and guitar were distinct
before 2500 B.C. (Plate IB.), and incurved sides were known
by 1000 B.C. (Plate III.). The origin of the guitar and
lute is to be found in the hunting bow, to which in the
first instance a gourd was attached as a resonator
(*cf.* H. Balfour, *The Natural History of the Musical
Bow*, 1899). In all probability the original Asiatic word
from which both *kithara* (for the lyre-form) and
kitar (for the guitar-form) are derived, was used
generally for any stringed instrument in much the same
way as the Greek *psalterion*. A very early instance of
the short-necked lute-form is provided by a pottery figure
discovered by Prof. Petrie in a Goshen cemetery (Saft-el-
Henna), and now in the Ashmolean Museum, Oxford.
The head of the instrument is slightly recurved, and the
work is said to date from the 18th to the 20th Egyptian
Dynasties (*c.* 1500-1000 B.C.), though it is a specimen of
foreign art, probably Minoan or early Greek (Plate IV.).

The first introduction of the guitar into Western
Europe seems to have come through the Romans, for in
the 13th century the *Chitarra Latina* (Guitare Latine),
with its short neck and flexuous outline, which gave to us
the Gittern and Cittern or Citole, was distinct from the
Chitarra Morisca (Guitare Moresque), a long-necked
instrument with an oval body, like those in Fig. 21, which
had been brought by the Moors into Spain. Both Greeks
and Romans were well acquainted with the various Guitar
forms of Western Asia (such as those they called the
Barbiton and the *Pandoura*), as extant illustrations in
their works of art plainly show.

CHAPTER II.

STRINGED INSTRUMENTS (*continued*).—THE NEBEL
AND NEBEL-AZOR.

THIS instrument will naturally present itself for
our consideration after the *kinnor*, not only because
it seems from all accounts to have been an
instrument of a more elaborated character, and
consequently of greater capabilities than the *kinnor*,
both as to tone and pitch, but also because it
appears in the Bible chronologically later. It is not
mentioned until 1 Sam. x. 5. This fact seems to
add weight to the opinion that it was of Phœnician
origin, inasmuch as the intercourse between
Phœnicia and Israel was not very close until about
that period. It is called "Sidonian" by the poet
quoted by Athenæus, lib. iv., c. 77—

"Οὖτε Σιδωνίον νάβλα
λαρυγγόφωνος ἐκκεχορδῶται τύπος."

In the Psalms and Nehemiah it is translated by
ψαλτήριον ("psaltery"), with the exception of
Ps. lxxi. 22, "I will also praise thee with the
psaltery, even thy truth, O my God," where the
word is ψαλμός; and also of Ps. lxxxi. 2, "Take a
psalm, bring hither the timbrel," where the Greek is

κιθάρα. With regard to the other places in Holy Scripture where it is mentioned, the Septuagint generally has it as ναβλίον, νάβλα, νάβλη, ναύλα, or νάβλας. As would be expected, the Latin forms are *nablium*, *nablum*, or *nabla*. In speaking of the *kinnor*, it was stated that that instrument was probably either a lyre or guitar; and those who assumed that the *kinnor* was the lyre, would imagine the *nebel* was the harp. Hence certain writers, amongst them Jerome, Cassiodorus, Isidorus, have believed the *nebel* to be of that simple form of harps, describing a mere Δ shape, which were given in Figs. 1 to 8. But on the other hand it must not be overlooked that the harp, like every other musical instrument, was undoubtedly improved from time to time, and the very fact of the comparative lateness of the allusion to the *nebel* in the Bible would suggest that it was of a somewhat more highly developed construction than that hinted at above. As regards simple and early forms of harps, some writers have laid great stress on the fact that the hollow resonance-box was held uppermost, and have in this way drawn a contrast between the harp and the guitar family. But this resolves itself into the plain question of the position in which the ancients held their harps when playing. That it was often different from our mode there can be no doubt, as is shown by such a representation as Fig. 19, copied from a Greek vase in the royal collection at Munich, which represents a female playing on a harp, having the resonance-box leaning against her shoulder. *See* also Fig. 7, p. 15.

But the most noticeable distinction between ancient and modern harps seems to be the almost

universal absence of a third side to the wooden
framework of the former.   This will be easily
observed by glancing at the various illustrations
of harps which have been and which will be given.

Fig. 19.

This third side forms a very important feature in
more modern instruments, and not only adds to the
strength of the instrument, but also allows the strings
to be drawn to a greater tension than could otherwise

be the case. In fact, it seems difficult to believe
how the woodwork, when consisting only of two sides,
could stand the strain upon it when the strings were
tuned. To those who have not given attention
to the subject this tension seems almost incredible.
In the case of a grand pianoforte, which contains
more strings than any other instrument in use, the
tension, it is calculated, approaches thirty tons.*

The third side of a harp is far from spoiling its
appearance. The harp shown in Fig. 20 is an
ancient Irish harp. One preserved in Trinity
College, Dublin, is popularly believed to have
belonged to the famous Brian Boiroimhe, who
ascended his throne 1001 A.D. But this tradition
has been ably controverted.† The illustration on
the next page was taken, by the kind permission of
the authorities of the Victoria and Albert Museum,
from the fine plaster cast in their possession, the
missing parts of the instrument being restored.

The word *nebel* is by some traced to a root
signifying a "rounded vase," or "leather bottle."
If this derivation be correct, we can imagine that
the instrument was conspicuous for the shape of

---

* The author's original note is interesting :—"To the kindness of
Mr. G. T. Rose, of Messrs. Broadwood, I am indebted for the fact
that when two pianofortes exhibited by that eminent firm in the
Exhibition of 1862 were tested with reference to this point, the tension
of one was 15 tons 9 cwt., of the other, 16 tons 11 cwt., both being
tuned to concert pitch. The greater weight representing the tension of
the latter instrument is accounted for by its being of a rather larger size;
of two strings, equal in other dimensions, but differing in length, the
longer will of course require a greater weight than the shorter, in order to
raise it to the *same* pitch."

Messrs. Broadwood have kindly informed me that at the present
time (1913) the tension of their full Concert Grand is 30 tons ; and to
Messrs. Steinway I am indebted for the statement that in their largest
instruments it is over 27 tons. For further particulars on this subject see
A. J. Hipkins, *History of the Pianoforte* (Novello).—ED.

† See Stoke's Life of Dr. Petrie, p. 318.

one of its sides, if it had two sides; or if it were curvilinear, from the form of the hollow framework. It is quite possible that it might have been like those delineated in Figs. 23, 24 and 25.*

But it is nearly always dangerous to argue from

Fig. 20,

the derivation of names of instruments. For instance, what could the musical historian of a thousand years hence gather of the construction of a harmonium, seraphine, accordion, or euphonium,

* See Supplementary Note (1), to this Chapter.

from the derivation of their respective names? Or, how much from the word "pianoforte," the "soft-loud!" Some have carried this misguiding principle so far as to say that because *nebel* was derived from "rounded vase" or "leather bottle," it would therefore answer the description of a *bagpipe!* This is, at least, an ingenious theory, but fortunately a well-defined title is given to the bagpipe (on the subject of which more will be said by-and-by), namely, *symphonia*, which renders this suggestion unworthy of consideration.

This is not the only theory as to the nature of a *nebel* which has been hazarded. Although it seems almost certain that it was a harp, some have suggested that it was a lute or guitar. But there is one very strong argument against this assumption that the *nebel* belonged to the family of guitars; it is this, that whereas the *nebel* is not infrequently mentioned in Roman and Greek authors, instruments with long necks seem to have been little recognized by them, or at most, to have been only known to them through actual specimens, or representations of them in sculpture, which had been captured and carried home.*

There is, however, indisputable proof that the Egyptians possessed such instruments, and Fig. 21 shows two women dancing to their own performance on such long-necked instruments.† The "necks" seem disproportionately prolonged in these examples, twice or three times the length of

---

* The kithara of the Greeks, it should be remembered, was in its construction a small *lyre*, not a guitar, although its name is so closely allied to that of the latter.

† This illustration is copied from an original sketch taken near Thebes by Lionel Muirhead, Esq., who kindly presented it to the author. See Supplementary Note (2), to this Chapter.

the body or resonance-box. But if Italian
instruments of this class, the lutes of the sixteenth
and seventeenth centuries, be examined, it will be
found that this relative proportion is not uncommon.
The great importance of these Egyptian lutes or
guitars, with reference to the progress of the science

Fig. 21.

as well as the art of music, must be our excuse for
a slight digression. It must have been known to
the players on these ancient instruments that their
fingers had always to squeeze down or "stop" the
strings at some definite place, in order to produce

certain intervals.* These distances were no doubt measured, and compared with each other, and with the whole length of the string. Thus indeed would the first foundation of the science of acoustics be laid, with all its interesting and important bearing on the art of music. And in order that the choice of the position of the finger should be found by the performer with greater certainty, *frets* were invented. Frets were originally pieces of gut (in the Egyptian instruments of camel-gut), tied round the neck, and so forming ridges on the finger-board at those places where the pressure of the fingers would cut off so much of the strings as should allow the vibrating portions to produce the successive notes of the scale. Thus, no doubt, the primary object of using frets was to secure a true production of the scale then in use, and at the same time to shorten and simplify the labour of the young student. But later in their history, when made of ebony or ivory, they had another important function. If the fingers of a grown man be placed side by side on the strings of a guitar, it will usually happen that they cover more space than the strings, or in other words, that there is not room for them in a straight line, each finger on a string. But the ridge made by a fret enables the performer to draw his fingers a little behind each other and yet play such a chord in tune. This will be understood by noticing the position of the tips of the fingers in Fig. 22 (*see* page 36). Mr. Chappell states† that the remains of frets were distinctly visible on some instruments found in an Egyptian tomb.

* See also the account of the Tamboura, in Engel's *Music of the most Ancient Nations*, pp. 52-57.

† *History of Music*, p. 44.

With regard to the possible relation of the *kinnor* to these Egyptian lutes or guitars, it may be said that if the *kinnor* assumed this form at all, it was probably less long in the neck, with a larger resonance-box (Plate IV.). The portability of the *kinnor*, to which its lengthened existence was greatly due, would certainly militate against the idea of its being constructed with three or four feet of fragile neck.

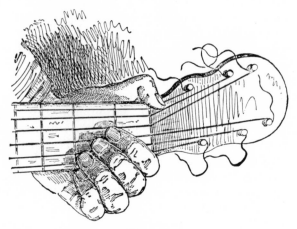

Fig. 22.

Assuming, then, that these interesting instruments were not identical with the *kinnor*, nor the *nebel*,—in the former case because of their fragile form, in the latter because they were unknown to nations who were familiar with the *nebel*,—we are led to the conclusion that the *nebel* itself was the veritable *harp* of the Hebrews. It could not have been large, because, as will be noticed later, it

is so frequently mentioned in the Bible as being
carried in processions.

The Egyptians and Assyrians had harps of
moderate size, as shown in Figs. 23, 24, and 25.

Very probably the *nebel* had a form similar to
the harp in Fig. 24, but with a somewhat more
rapid curve. It would in this way be rendered
more portable.

Fig. 23.

Before noticing some of the most important
passages in the Bible in which *nebels* are mentioned,
it is necessary to point out that the English translators render *nebel* (apparently without any special
reason) by no less than four different words:
(1) Psaltery, (2) Psalm, (3) Lute, (4) Viol. The
first of these is by far the most common in the

authorised version, and is no doubt the most correct translation if the word be understood in its true sense as a *portable harp*.

Nebels, like *kinnors*, were made of fir-wood, and afterwards of almug.*   Samuel told the newly-anointed king Saul that he would meet " a company

Fig. 24.

of prophets coming down from the high place with a *nebel*" and other musical instruments.   And afterwards " David and all the house of Israel played before the Lord on all manner of instruments made of fir-wood, even on *kinnors* and on *nebels*," &c.   On the happy event of the fetching of the Ark from

* Almug, or algum, perhaps the red *sandal-wood* of India.   See *Plants of the Bible*, by Sir John Hooker.   (Spottiswoode's *Sunday School Teachers' Bible*.)

Kirjath-jearim, " David and all Israel played before God with all their might " on *kinnors*, *nebels*, and timbrels. In 1 Chron. xv. the names of the players on *nebels* are carefully recorded. It is evident that David himself was as proficient on the *nebel* as on the *kinnor*, and that he set aside special players for special instruments (1 Chron. xxv. 1, &c.). In the Book of Psalms frequent mention is

Fig. 25.

made of the *nebel* (Ps. xxxiii. 2 ; lvii. 8 ; lxxi. 22 ; lxxxi. 2 ; xcii. 3 ; cviii. 2 ; cxliv. 9 ; cl. 3). It was not restricted in its use to religious ceremonies: Isaiah complains, " The *kinnor*, and the *nebel*,* the tabret, and pipe, and wine are in their feasts " (Isa. v. 12); and similarly Amos writes, " Take thou away from me the noise of thy songs ; for I will not

---

* Here translated *viol*.

hear the melody of thy *nebels* "* (Amos v. 23), and he prophesies woe on them that " lie on beds of ivory," " eat the lambs out of the flock," "chant to the sound of the *nebel*,"* and "drink wine in bowls " (Amos vi. 4-6).　In old English translations of Psalm lxxxi. 2 the *nebel* is called a " viol."　But it must be understood that in these passages the translators used

Fig. 26.

the word inadvertently, and not in the least wishing to suggest that the Hebrews had an instrument commonly played with a bow.

It is remarkable that the *nebel* is frequently mentioned in conjunction with some other musical instrument : for instance, with the *toph* (tambour),

* Here translated *viol.*

shophar (trumpet), &c. It may not be unfair to argue from this that its tones were deep and heavy, and were best adapted to form the groundwork of other combinations of various qualities and pitch.

The instrument shown in Fig. 26 seems to be a very early type of harp, and as such is interesting.

The negro harp, or *nanga* (Fig. 27), is probably of great antiquity, and to this day retains the same original form.

This remarkable instrument seems almost to

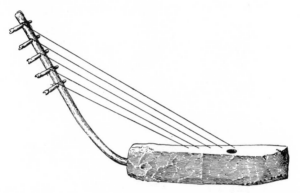

Fig. 27.

suggest that *all* string-instruments may have been evolved from one type, namely, strings stretched across a bent stick, as originally suggested to our earliest forefathers by their hunting-bows. But of this we shall speak later on.

A very peculiar form of small harp is shown in Fig. 28, which is copied from an Assyrian stone in the British Museum. Carl Engel, whose opinions were nearly always most trustworthy, seems in this case to have somewhat ventured on a mere speculation when he named this the *azor*, a word about which we shall next speak. The *plectrum* in the player's right hand is very evident; and also the curious termination of one of the sides in the form of a hand, perhaps used for holding the music, as is a small brass lyre or other contrivance in our modern military instruments.

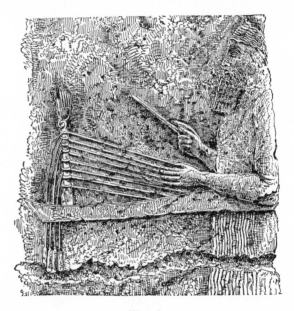

Fig. 28.

With *nebel* is often associated the word *azor*, which is traced to a root signifying *ten*, and which has therefore been rendered in the Septuagint by ἐν δεκαχόρδῳ or as ψαλτήριον δεκάχορδον (*psalterium decem chordarum*, or, *in dechachordo psalterio* in the Vulgate). In the Chaldee, Syriac, and Arabic versions also are found words implying the existence of ten strings in the *nebel-azor*.*

The word *azor* may therefore be considered as qualifying or describing the special kind of *nebel* to be used, much in the same way as we now speak of a *trichord* pianoforte. It is in our English version always rendered by the words " ten-stringed." In Ps. cxliv. 9 the associated word *nebel* is wrongly translated *lute* instead of *harp* in the Prayer-book version.

SUPPLEMENTARY NOTES.

(1.) In ancient days the harp assumed two distinct forms: the typical *Egyptian* harp was bow-shaped and the typical *Assyrian* harp was triangular, both forms being without the front pillar, which is so important a feature in the modern European instrument. These two kinds of harp seem to have been used by the Hebrews. The earliest, as we should naturally expect, was the bow-shaped instrument of Egypt, so frequently depicted in the frescoes and especially connected with the religious worship of that country: for it was the instrument of Egypt *par excellence*, and is represented in the hands of their deities, like the transverse flute of the Hindoo Siva. Illustrations of it occur which date long before the Shepherd Invasion and the settlement of Semitic families in Egypt some 2,500 years before our era. In process of time this harp developed from the three-, four-, or seven-stringed instrument of early days, which could be carried shoulder-high by women (Fig. 26), to fine instruments with from eleven to twenty or more strings (Figs. 23, 24, 29, 30). I agree with Dr. Stainer that the *nebel* was probably a harp of this form, and that it shared its natural development. For at the outset, the Egyptian harp must have consisted merely of a bow with a gourd attached to give greater resonance to the string.

* See Supplementary Note (1), to this Chapter.

The gourd is the popular water-bottle of the East, and hence the name *nebel*, which in its original sense means "a withered or dry thing"—therefore such a dry, empty thing as a gourd seed-vessel or "bottle." Nor does it cause us surprise to find that the Israelites, when in Egypt, did not employ the harp; for their own religious scruples and the sanctity of the instrument in the eyes of the Egyptians would have prevented it. When, however, they had been settled for many years in their own land, its use was not only possible but natural, and it is instructive to observe that it is mentioned for the first time in connection with one of their own religious establishments, that of the prophets (1 Samuel x. 5), and in its early portable form. Shortly afterwards it takes its place in the Temple worship.

In later Hebrew history there appears the other form of Oriental harp—the *nebel-azor*, an instrument with ten strings, as the suffix *azor* is said to imply. But the word in English should be spelt "asor," and, in my own opinion, it is quite likely that it is a dialectical or a mistaken corruption of the word *ashor*, for the Hebrew letter *shin* (ש) was anciently without distinction and used equally for "sh" and "s," whilst *aleph* (א) and *ain* (ע), with which the two words respectively commence, were frequently interchanged. If so, the original name meant the *Assyrian* harp, of which we have an illustration in Fig. 25, and a model in the little wooden statuette, probably from Thebes, shown on Plate V. (Brit. Mus.).

To the Greeks and Romans the bow-shaped harp of Egypt was known as the *nabla*, and although, as mentioned by Dr. Stainer, a Sidonian origin was attributed to it, it probably arose from the simple fact that it was first introduced to them by Phœnician traders; for, on the ribs (πλευρά) of the *nabla* of which the poet Mustakos sings in the quotation given by Athenaeus (Book iv., ch. 77), the lotus flower of Egypt was painted in the same way as it is on the harps shown in the ancient Egyptian wall-pictures (Fig. 24). In a fresco found at Pompeii, now in the Museo Nazionale, Naples, a lady is seen tuning her lyre to the bow-shaped *nabla* by her side. In fact, the

V. THE TRIANGULAR HARP.—EGYPTIAN ART: *c.* 1300 B.C. (p. 44.)

name *nanga*, still given to a very similar instrument in the region of the Upper Nile (Fig. 27), is probably only a nasalised corruption of the classical *nabla* and the Hebrew *nebel*.

(2.) The identification of the *nebel* with the harp is rendered easier if we dismiss from our minds the suggestion made both by Engel (*Music of the most Ancient Nations*) and Chappell (*History of Music*) that its name is a transliteration of the Egyptian word *nefer* which, from the shape of its hieroglyphic, is supposed to have been the name of the long-necked guitar shown in Fig. 21, though no actual application of the word in this connection is forthcoming. Modern Egyptologists, including Professor Flinders Petrie, consider that this hieroglyphic sign, which means "good," represents the heart and the tracheæ. It is not unlikely that the Egyptians believed that the wind-pipe (and therefore the power of speech) was connected with the heart, an idea common in ancient times and alluded to in the well-known words of the New Testament, "Out of the abundance of the heart the mouth speaketh. A good man out of the good treasure of the heart bringeth forth good things: and an evil man out of the evil treasure bringeth forth evil things " (Matt. xii. 34, 35). Mr. F. L. Griffith (*Hieroglyphs*, 1898) admits that the markings on the body of the sign for "good" are similar to those on that denoting the heart. Another detail, pointed out by Dr. Biernath (*Die Guitarre*, 1907) is that the one cross-bar (as in the earlier form of the hieroglyph), or the two cross-bars (as in the later), though they suggest to us the idea of tuning-pegs inserted in the side of the neck, have no counterpart in the Egyptian representations of the instrument itself. Neither in their drawings of guitar-players nor in an actual specimen of the instrument discovered at Thebes is there any trace of tuning-pegs: the two or three strings are wound round the top of the neck, the ends hanging loose, just as is still found in some of the more primitive guitars and lutes of Upper Africa. In these examples the strings are strained as tightly as possible before being wound round the neck, and closer tuning is effected by a loop of cord or leather, which slides up and down the fingerboard and binds the strings to it. It is more likely that the single cross-bar of the hieroglyph represents the mouth, and the double cross-bars the open lips.

Considering then that this ancient sign has nothing to do with a musical instrument, I may add that the long-necked guitar, for which so great an antiquity has been hitherto claimed in Egypt, was only introduced with other refinements of the East at the beginning of the New Empire (*c.* 1580 B.C.), when even Babylonia was paying tribute to the Pharaohs and the Egyptian fleet was traversing the Indian Ocean: for the first illustrations of the instrument appear in the opening years of that powerful XVIIIth Dynasty. Are the Burmese indebted to the enterprise of that time or to the agency of later Arab traders for their unique little harp called *soung*, so like the bow-shaped harp of Egypt? (Plate VI.)

That the Hebrews, however, should have remained unacquainted with this Oriental lute or guitar, pictured in the carvings of Assyria as early as 2500 B.C. (Plate I., B), and in Hittite sculpture before 1000 B.C. (Plate III.), appears most improbable, and there can be little doubt that the word *shalishim* (1 Sam. xviii. 6) meaning "three," and translated in the margin of the Authorised Version "three-stringed instruments," denotes this guitar, which was known to the Greeks as the *pandoura* and to the peoples of the Eastern Mediterranean countries of to-day as the *tanboura*. Dr. Stainer's contention (p. 182) that the passage, referred to above, requires that *all* the women of Israel should have been experts on the *shalish* is beyond the mark, though we shall agree with him that it was not a fiddle they played. Alike amongst the Assyrians, the Egyptians, and the Hittites, the *tanboura* was pre-eminently a Volk-instrument, as I myself recently had an opportunity of observing in modern Egypt and Palestine. Used by the women for song and dance, it is only natural that although the instrument found no place in the Ritual of the Temple, it was common enough in the Israelitish home, and

VI.   THE BOW-SHAPED HARP (SOUNG), BURMAH.   (p. 46.)

frequently associated with the rhythmic beat of the small hand-drum (*toph*). The popularity of the long-necked guitar in the ordinary life of ancient Egypt is quaintly illustrated by some rude but spirited paintings executed by a much later hand on the walls of a pre-historic tomb at Hierakonpolis. The fine surface evidently afforded an excellent opportunity for practice, and, amongst the boats, wild creatures, and human forms here depicted at random, there are three musicians performing on the guitar, undoubtedly the instrument most familiar to the young artist. The paintings are reproduced in the *Egyptian Research Account*, 5th Memoir, "Hierakonpolis," Part II., Pl. 77, by Quibell & Green (London, 1902).

An interesting illustration of this long-necked lute or guitar has just been discovered on a sculptured slab, unearthed by Professor Hogarth, under the auspices of the British Museum, at Jerablus, in Syria, the site of the ancient Hittite city of Carchemish. The instrument is being played by an attendant in a sacrificial scene, and the date of the slab is said to be the 12th cent. B.C.

The Hebrew word *minnim*, which literally means "divided out," and is supposed to denote instruments with strings set out in an ordered row, like the harp, may, however, have a special reference to the frets or divisions on the neck of the *shalish*, if, as I conclude, it was identical with the *tanboura* of the present day.

CHAPTER III.

STRINGED INSTRUMENTS *(continued).*—SABECA AND
PSANTERIN.

Sabeca is one of the instruments mentioned
as being used in the well-known band of
Nebuchadnezzar, as described in Dan. iii. 5. It
was therefore not a Hebrew, but a Babylonish,
instrument. It is most unfortunately translated
" sackbut " in our version. This is to be regretted,
because not only does sackbut possess no relation
whatever to *sabeca,* but also it is itself a word the
meaning and the application of which are surrounded
with much obscurity. The sackbut of Europe
was certainly a kind of bass trumpet, in fact, a
trombone. But although we have before this given
warning of the danger likely to arise from
attempting to describe instruments from the
derivation of their names, it is impossible to
disregard an interpretation which at first sight
seems obvious and undisputed: for the root *sac,*
signifying a pouch or bag, runs through a vast
number of languages—Hebrew, Arabic, and most
of the European languages dead or now used;
and there is also, according to some, a root *boog* in
Arabic, and *buk* in Hebrew, meaning a " trumpet "

or "pipe." Hence arises the great temptation to jump to the conclusion that a sackbut must have been a "bagpipe," especially as the German name for a bagpipe is *Sackpfeife*, which looks as if it were a near relation to "sackbut." On the other hand it is difficult to account for the application of such a term as "bag-trumpet" to a trombone, an instrument which differs very slightly, if at all, from a trumpet in the general form of its outline. The fact, however, remains unshaken that the European sackbut was a trombone, the word being used in the same sense in many languages, as, for instance, in old French, *saqueboute*, and in Italian, *sacabuche.** The reader must forgive this digression on a word which, as has been remarked, ought not to have found its way into our translation of the Book of Daniel. The *sabeca*, then, which is *not* a sackbut, is generally identified with the σάμβυξ or σαμβύκη, *sambuca*, a harp known to the Greeks and Romans as an ingredient of Oriental luxury. They were evidently played upon by men as well as by women, as a player on the *sambuca* is a σαμβυκιστής or σαμβυκίστρια, *sambucistus* or *sambucistria*. But, granting that the *sabeca* was a *sambuca*, the question is, what was a *sambuca*? Two answers are given. One, that it was a very small harp of high pitch; the other, that it was a large harp with a great many strings. Both statements may be true of different periods of its existence. That the term was once applied to a small *trigon* (possibly when made of elder-wood, *sambucus*) is unquestionable; but there are also authors who have identified it with many instruments of a far more important development. It is more probable, therefore, that

* See Chapter viii., Supplementary Note (1).

it was a large and powerful harp, of a rich quality
of tone. Some have thought it very similar to, if
not identical with, the great Egyptian harp, and
have considered the next illustrations (Figs. 29, 30)
as representations of it.*

It will be well, perhaps, to state here what were
the instruments mentioned in Dan. iii. 5, 7, 10, 15.
They were (1) *keren*, a horn (σάλπιγξ); (2) *mashrokitha*,
pan's-pipes or small organ (σῦριγξ); (3) *kithara*,
a lyre (κιθάρα); (4) *sabeca*, a triangular harp (σαμβύκη);

Fig. 29.   Fig 30.

(5) *psanterin*, a psaltery (ψαλτήριον); (6) *symphonia*,
a bagpipe (συμφωνία).   In the succeeding chapters
an account of each of these instruments will be
found.

PSANTERIN.

The consideration of this instrument will lead us
into much that is interesting. The *psanterin*,
pesanterin, or *phsanterin* (Dan. iii. 5, 7, 10, 15), has

---

* For other examples of such instruments the reader is referred to the
Appendix to F. von Drieberg's *Wörterbuch der Griechischen Musik.* (Berlin,
1835.)   Also see Supplementary Note (1), to this Chapter.

been translated in the Septuagint by the word
ψαλτήριον (*psalterion*), *psalterium*, and although
rendered "psaltery" in the English version, it
may have been a *dulcimer*. Perhaps no instrument
has undergone less changes, or been of more
widespread use, than the dulcimer. When, therefore, in our own villages we have seen the
itinerant rustic musician place one on a table or
stool and rap out a merry tune, we have really seen
a modern counterpart of the instrument which was
used in that terrible ordeal when the faithful
worshippers had, at the peril of a fiery death, to
pronounce their sublime belief in an unseen God
in opposition to the grovelling veneration of wood,
stone, or gold; and when they boldly stood forth, a
mere handful of righteous men, in the midst of a
mighty idolatrous nation. One can hardly realise
the awfulness of the scene, the intense anxiety on
all faces, when, as the music broke forth, a signal
for all to bend to the golden image, those "three
children" stood unmoved, upright. When the
sounds of harps, trumpets, and bagpipes gathered
on the ear, to which these simple "psalteries" added
their share, how every eye must have been strained
to catch a glimpse of those strange believers in the
Unseen!

The custom of causing a loud crash of musical
sounds to accompany any tragic scene has survived
amongst many savage nations, torture and execu-
tions being not unfrequently accompanied by the
noisiest attainable music.

It must be carefully borne in mind that the word
"psaltery" is generally used as a translation of
nebel, but no confusion need arise if it be
remembered that mention of the *psanterin* is *only*

to be found in Dan. iii. 5, 7, 10, 15. That the word "psaltery" should have been somewhat loosely used by the learned translators of the Bible is not surprising when we remember that the verb ψάλλω (*psallo*) signifies "to play upon a harp or lyre," that ψάλτης (*psaltes*) is a male harpist, and ψάλτρια (*psaltria*) a female harpist. And, moreover, so thoroughly is this class of words connected with harp- or lyre-playing, that the very title of the Book of "Psalms" is given to it because it is a collection of songs to be sung to the accompaniment of a harp or lyre. And still more, in ecclesiastical Latin, *psallere* not unfrequently means " to sing the Psalms of David." *Psanterin* is unquestionably connected with the Chaldee *santeer ;* but Villoteau, quoted by Fétis, goes on to say that the Egyptians would affix to it the article *pi*, making it *pisanteer ;* and, again, that the Assyrians would suffix *in*, making the whole *pisanterin;* whence *psanterin* or *phsanterin.* Villoteau is, however, wrong, for on the authority of a sound Semitic scholar I am enabled to say that there is no Assyrian termination *in*, and that in the transfer of the word from the Greek to the *Chaldee, l* and *n* would be interchanged, and the termination *ion* would either be converted into *in* or be dropped out altogether ; also, as the compound letter *ps* (ψ) is not represented in Arabic, the word would become *santerin* or *santeer*, perhaps more properly written *santyr.* The mention, in the above-named quotation from the Book of Daniel, of several other instruments whose Chaldee names have a very similar sound to their Greek translations —namely, *keren* (κέρας), horn; *kithros* (κιθάρα), lyre ; and especially *symphonia* (συμφωνία), bag-pipe— forces us to believe that these names were actually borrowed from the Greek. The intercourse between Asia and Greece, through Phœnicia, would be sufficient to account for this. But on the other hand it seems very remarkable, if the above supposition be correct, that the *orchestra* (as we should term it) on such an important ceremony in Babylon should consist entirely of *foreign* instruments. The arguments on both sides are to be found in many of our best critical commentaries on the Bible.

The word *psalterion* is, as before remarked, formed from *psallo*, which is a strengthened form of ψάω *(psao)*, and signifies "to touch on the surface, to stroke." To many of our readers an apology may be necessary for entering into such well-known details; but it is felt that to some, into whose hands this little book may chance to come, such information may not be uninteresting or useless. A word derived from this ψάω has been aptly used for the *twitch* which a carpenter gives to a coloured or chalked string when he wishes it to leave a mark. This is highly suggestive of the action of lyre or harp playing; it is not strange, therefore, that when used in a musical sense, the word should imply *plucking with the fingers*, as opposed to striking with a *plectrum* or *style*, which latter was as common or more common a practice among the ancients than the former.

Our word "dulcimer" seems on good authority to have been derived from the Italian, perhaps from the old word *dolcimela*, which is connected with *dolcin*. Now *dolcin* is a kind of *oboe*; but it must not be thought that any relationship whatever to the oboe was suggested by the title "dulcimer." This is but one more proof of the

utter confusion which is to be found in the
application of musical terms; or rather, perhaps,
suggests the intimate connection which has existed
between all phases of musical history.*   The word
dolcin survives to this day in the catalogues of the
registers or stops in old German organs, appearing
as *dolcan, dulcan, dulcian,* or *dulzian,* and signifying
generally either a deep oboe or high bassoon.
From this source we get our *dulciana,* the name of
the lovely soft-toned stop invented by Snetzler, the
eighteenth-century builder of many fine organs in
different parts of England.   The Spanish have the
exact counterpart of this word in their *dulcaynas,*
mentioned in *Don Quixote,* where deep-toned
oboes are evidently meant, and where they are
ascribed to a Moorish origin.   *Dulciana* is, however,
not wisely applied to Snetzler's organ-stop, as it
consists of flue-, not reed-pipes.

The earliest form of the dulcimer was of the
rudest description, probably a flat piece of wood,
generally four-sided, either rectangular or with two
converging sides, having strings attached to fixed
pins on one side, and to movable tuning-pins on
the other.   Then, in process of time, the simple
flat piece of wood was found to be capable of
conversion into a resonance-box, and the dulcimer
became a genuine stringed instrument constructed
without a neck, because, inasmuch as the strings
were hit with little hammers held in the hand, the
long neck became a useless extension.

Then, again, the strings would be made, on the
inner side of the pins, to pass over a bridge, either

---

* See also in Chapter ix. an account of the association of the word *cymbal*
(cembalo) with the dulcimer, and the Supplementary Notes to this
Chapter and to Chapter ix.

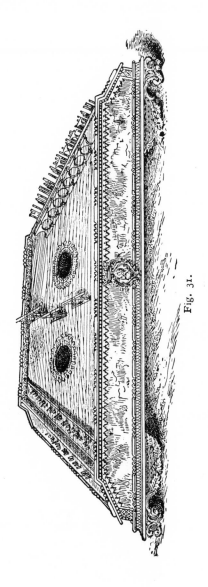

Fig. 31.

as a continuous bridge running parallel to the converging sides, or as separate movable bridges

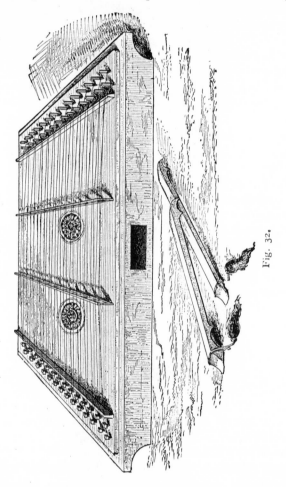

Fig. 32.

under each string. Then, again, in order to produce a greater volume of tone, more than one string came to be allotted to one note, several strings, perhaps as many as three or four, tuned of course in unison, being grouped to each note. In nearly all cases the instrument is now played upon by little hammers, one being wielded by each hand of the performer. The German name of the dulcimer, *hackbret* (chopping-board), is eminently expressive of the position and action of the player. It is important to note that the Italian name of the instrument is *salterio* (Fig. 31), as this word connects the Greek ψαλτήριον with the modern European instruments. By some strange fatality the translators of the Authorised Version have dragged in the word "dulcimer" as a translation of *symphonia* (συμφωνία), and not of *psanterin* (ψαλτηριον) ; so the last three instruments mentioned in our version are these : sackbut, psaltery, dulcimer ; whereas they should read, harp (*sabeca*), psaltery or dulcimer (*psanterin*), bagpipe (*symphonia*). Fig. 32 illustrates a Chinese dulcimer, called by them *yang-kin*. It is played with two little sticks ; the strings, which are of brass, are very thin. On this instrument, Carl Engel (by whose learning and persevering research the public interest in these subjects, which culminated in the valuable collection at South Kensington, was aroused) has said : — " The resemblance of the *yang-kin* to our dulcimer, and to the *santir* of the Arabs and Persians, is very remarkable, and suggests various conjectures." The *kin*, another Chinese instrument, which is of a long oblong shape, with a curved sound-board, is improperly called the "scholar's lute," because it was the favourite instrument of Confucius. When played it is, like the dulcimer, placed upon a table ;

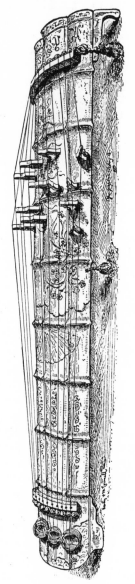

Fig. 33.

but, unlike the dulcimer, the strings are twanged with the fingers, instead of being struck with hammers or sticks ; and, also, the strings are made to produce several notes by being pressed down by the fingers at given points, or, as we technically term it, by being " stopped." The Japanese have instruments called *goto*, or *koto*, which are of the same class ; that shown in Fig. 33 is a *sono-koto*, made of kiri-wood, having movable bridges which of course enable a performer to tune it to several distinct successions of intervals or scales. It is played with " plectra " (*tsumé*) fixed on the finger-tips of the right hand, while the left hand, by pressing the sounding string on the other side of the bridge, produces sharps, grace-notes, and " tremolo " effects. The long strings, thirteen in number, are of carefully-twisted silk. To this instrument the Chinese *tsang* or *tche* bears a remarkable resemblance, not only in shape, but in having movable bridges. The next illustration (Fig. 34) is a *santir* of Georgia, of very elegant construction, being made of wood inlaid with mother-of-pearl. It has twenty-three sets of wire strings, three strings tuned in unison making up each set.

The handsome instrument depicted on page 55 is an Italian dulcimer or *salterio* of the middle of the 18th century. The comparison of this, with that shown in Fig. 34, will lead to the most interesting results. One more illustration will be given, and then it is hoped the reader will have had sufficient proof of the connection between the *salterio* of Europe, derived from *psalterium*, and the *santir* of the East, derived from *psanterin* (Fig. 31 showing the *salterio*, Fig. 34 the *santir*).

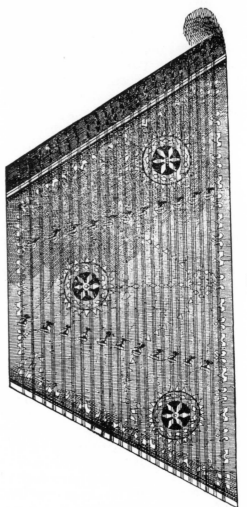

Fig. 34.

The Indian specimen illustrated on the next page (Fig. 35) is the *sar mundal* of Benares. An instrument of a similar shape and appearance, and having the tuning-pins arranged in the same way, is the *kanoon*, which Engel says is an especial favourite with the ladies of Turkey. Its strings are of gut, and are twanged with a plectrum of tortoise-shell pointed with cocoanut-shell. An Egyptian instrument of like construction has been described by Lane (*Modern Egyptians*, ch. xviii.). The Hindoos call the *sar mundal* the "hundred-stringed Vina."

It is worthy of remark that the early English instrument was called *sautrie* or *sawtry*, an evident corruption of "psaltery." Allusions to this in old writers are sufficiently numerous. Chaucer, in describing the charms and accomplishments of Nicholas, the Oxford student, and the furniture of his room, says :—

> '' And all above there lay a gay sautrie,
> On which he made on nightes melodie
> So swetely that all the chambre rong :
> And *Angelus ad Virginem* he song.''

Fortunately a contemporaneous account of this instrument is to be found in Bartholomæus' *De Proprietatibus Rerum*, written originally in Latin, and translated in 1398. It is given by Hawkins (*History of Music*, ch. lx.) as follows :—

DE PSALTERIO.

" The sawtry highte Psalterium, and hath that name of *psallendo*, syngynge; for the consonant answeryth to the note thereof in syngynge. The harpe is like to the sawtry in sowne. But this is the dyuersytee and discorde bytwene the harpe and the sawtry : in the sawtry is an holowe tree, and of that same tree the sowne comyth upwarde, and the strynges ben smytte downwarde and sownyth upward ; and in the harpe the holownesse of the tre is bynethe. . . Stringes for the sawtry ben

Fig. 35.

beste made of laton,* or elles those ben goode that ben made of syluer."

But instruments of the dulcimer family are not only interesting to us as being used over such a wide geographical area, and among nations of such various types, but also as being the forerunners of that most useful, as it is too one of the most

* *Laton* or *latten*, " yellow metal " : an alloy of copper and zinc, like brass.

beautiful, of modern instruments—the pianoforte. Imagine a dulcimer the hammers of which are made to strike by means of keys, or *claves*, and a miniature pianoforte is the result. There seems to be some doubt as to whether a system of keys was first applied to the organ or to a stringed instrument. The leap from a dulcimer to a pianoforte would have been immediate, if the first instruments with keyboards had been provided with " falling " hammers wherewith to strike the strings.

But the *clavichord*, *clarichord*, or *monochord*, which was apparently the first attempt, had as its chief characteristic a brass pin or tangent at the end of the key which not only set the string in vibration, but by resting against it portioned off the part which was to vibrate. Much information is given on the subject of this instrument in Dr. Rimbault's well-known work on the history of the pianoforte.* And simple as this system seems to us, the clavichord held its own till the time of J. S. Bach, that marvellous man whose instinctive mastery of the art of music has made his works the treasure-house of all accomplished musicians to this day, albeit he was born in 1685 ! His son, C. P. E. Bach, played on one to Dr. Burney.

Another form which these early keyed-stringed instruments took was that of the *clavicytherium*, or keyed cithara, a small oblong box containing strings which, when the keys were pressed down, were plucked by quills. The tone produced in this manner has been aptly described as " a scratch with a sound at the end of it." Yet this peculiar twang, though not always similarly produced, was

---

* See also " A History of the Pianoforte and of the older Keyboard Instruments," by A. J. Hipkins (Novello's Music Primers).

not only borne with, but delighted in, from about the 13th century to the beginning of the 19th—a most lasting popularity.

The quill was placed into a small slip of wood, called a "jack," in such a manner that as the jack rose, the quill plucked the string; but as it fell again, the quill passed by the string, and remained ready for another stroke. Bits of cloth were used as dampers—that is, they stopped the vibration of a string when the key was allowed to rise, with the same result as in a modern pianoforte. The *virginal* and *spinet* were two instruments of this

Fig. 36.

class, the first so called because the favourite of ladies, or, as some say, in compliment to Queen Elizabeth; the latter from the resemblance of the quill plucker or plectrum to a thorn (*spina*). They seem to have differed from each other only in shape, the former being made oblong, the latter three-sided, or the shape of a harp lying down. Engravings of both are given (see Figs. 36 and 37).

These were to be in time rivalled by the *cembalo*, or *harpsichord*, which included many improvements, such, for instance, as the formation of two rows of keys, mechanical contrivances for causing each key to play the octave above, or octave below, its own sound.

Fig. 37.

On the cases of all the instruments just described, our forefathers were wont to bestow much decoration. In many examples, when the lid was thrown open for the performer, its inner side disclosed an elegant oil-painting, a landscape, or symbolical figures. Some were very richly inlaid with various woods, or even with precious stones. In this utilitarian age we pride ourselves (a little too much, perhaps) on giving consideration to the tone, and disregarding the appearance of the case.

The harpsichord is by no means to be despised as a musical instrument; for although vastly inferior in quality and quantity of tone to a grand pianoforte, it possesses a remarkable power of variety, and can be either bright and sparkling, or rich and sonorous in sound. On such an instrument did Handel practise, or while away his time, or perchance draw out the threads of some of his grand conceptions. The fact that the pianoforte did not at first receive sufficient public favour to enable it to displace the harpsichord accounts for the overlapping of the history of the two. The highly-finished harpsichord was no doubt superior to the tentative pianoforte : we can therefore fully sympathise with the public feeling of that day.

It will, it is hoped, have been observed by the reader that the word *psaltery* in its classical sense of a *harp*, is quite a justifiable translation of the Hebrew word *nebel*, but in its modern sense (associated with the Italian *salterio*) it is a more proper translation of *psanterin*—a dulcimer. That ψαλτήριον (psalterion) should have been used in the Septuagint for both *nebel* and *psanterin* is much to be regretted. But, as before remarked, its use as a translation of *psanterin* is limited to the Book of Daniel.

SUPPLEMENTARY NOTES.

(1.) Vitruvius (*De Architecturâ*, Book 6) informs us that in shape the *sambuca* was triangular and of true geometrical form: Andreas of Panormo, quoted by Athenaeus (Book xiv., ch. 33), says that it was like a ship and a ladder combined. If therefore we take the triangular instrument so frequently represented in Assyrian sculpture (Fig. 28) as the earlier model of the *sambuca*, it is very probable that the substitution of tuning pegs (Fig. 8) for sliding loops on the vertical rod gave to later writers the idea of a ladder, while the horizontal and hollow resonator suggested the boat or ship. There is no reason to think that the instrument was necessarily made of elder wood, as, from its Greek and Latin names, has been stated. The *m* in *sambuca* is merely a phonetic insertion, which often occurs in words derived from other languages. The original is *sabeca*, in Syrian *sabka*. Dr. Stainer is right in thinking that, as time progressed, it received a greater elaboration: the *lyrophoenix* or Phoenician lyre was an improved *sambuca*, and the addition of a rigid support between the top of the vertical rod and the end of the resonator may have suggested the well-known triangular-framed harp (*trigon*).

(2.) Dr. Stainer has throughout this chapter lost sight of the marked difference between the mediæval psaltery and dulcimer. Although so similar in shape and construction, the psaltery was plucked by the fingers or swept by a plectrum, whereas the dulcimer is struck by small hammers. In the Assyrian carvings the use of the plectrum with the triangular harp (*sabeca*) is clearly seen (Fig. 28); but no ancient representation of the true psaltery—an instrument in which strings are stretched over and across a soundbox—is as yet forthcoming, much less that of a dulcimer. Engel's "Assyrian dulcimer" (*Music of the most Ancient Nations*, p. 44) is in reality a triangular harp of the kind already described, but

" improved " by a recent European restorer in his attempt
to mend the cracked condition of the ancient slab on
which it appears. The true *psaltery* seems to have
originated in Northern or in Eastern Asia, for it is seen in
the Chinese *kin* and *tche*, for which a remote antiquity
is claimed, and also in the *koto* (Fig. 33), the national
instrument of Japan. The dulcimer is represented in
China only by the *yang-kin* or " foreign kin " (Fig. 32),
a name which shows that it is considered a recent
importation : it is said, from Italy. The Indian *svarman-
dala* or *sar mundal* (Fig. 35) and the popular Asiatic
kanoon are still plucked by the fingers or by little plectra,
and are therefore psalteries ; whereas the Persian *santir*
and that of Georgia (Fig. 34) are now struck with small
curved sticks, as dulcimers. It seems probable therefore
that the instrument in which the strings are struck, and
which requires a stronger framework, first came into use
in Western Asia, as far as we know about the eighth or
ninth century of our era : it was popularised in Europe
by the Crusades, and its sweet tone won for it the epithet
doucemelle (*dulce melos*), whence its present name is
derived. It was also called the *cembalo* or *cymbal* from
the similarity of its sound and manner of playing to the
bell-chimes called cymbals (*cf.* Chapter ix., Supplementary
Note (1)). In France the title *tympanon* was given to the
dulcimer because it was *struck ;* but in Italy the name of
its predecessor was retained, though qualified as the
salterio tedesco or the " German " psaltery.

CHAPTER IV.

KITHROS, *cithara* (κιθάρα), is one of the instruments mentioned in Dan. iii. 5, 7, 10, 15 : the Greek form of the name, as before remarked, strengthens the argument that the instrument itself was a foreign importation. In Ezek. xxvii., the prophet, in giving the many sources of luxury and greatness open to Tyre, distinctly alludes to Grecian traffic ; and, moreover, in the succeeding age to the fall of Troy Æolian and Ionian colonies were transplanted into Asia. There is, therefore, more than one channel through which Greek names of musical instruments could become familiar in Asia. From the Latin *cithara* our word *guitar* is derived, but this is only one of a large family of words sprung from a common origin. The Arabians have their *kuitra*, a kind of lute ; the Persians, *kitar*, a long-necked guitar. The Nubian *kissar*, which is a lyre, has already been described, but it may be well to add that the Egyptians call the *kissar* " gytarah barbaryeh," or the Berbers' guitar.* In Europe the name has undergone many changes ; the old French form is *guiterne* ; the old English, *gittern*,

* See p. 22.

cithern, cither, cythorn, or *gythorn;* Italian, *ghiterra* or *chiterra (chitarrone,* a big cithara, was a long-necked theorbo or bass lute) ; German, *zither,* but this is not the instrument now called by this name. It is remarkable that Sanskrit *katur* means *four,*

Fig. 38.

and that *chutara* in Persian may mean four strings, and also that the Hindus have a name implying a numerical value, *si-tar,* "the three-stringed," * which is given to a very popular instrument with three strings and a long neck, invented, it is said,

* *Cf.* Supplementary Note (2), Chapter i.

in the 12th century A.D., but in reality an offshoot of the ancient Asiatic *tanboura*.

As a lyre and a guitar have been depicted in Figs. 17 and 18, pages 23, 25, and the upper part of the neck of a modern European guitar in Fig. 22, page 36, it will only be necessary now to give some

Fig. 39.

illustrations of old *kitharas*, which are simply elaborated lyres possessing greater resonance and musical capabilities (see Figs. 38, 39, 40, 41, 42).

Fig. 41, which appears in a painting discovered at Herculaneum, is remarkable in that there are evidently two strings to each note.

Some authors have affirmed that without doubt the Hebrews had *kitharas* of this classical form, and appeal in proof of their assertion to the devices on Maccabæan medals shown in Figs. 43, 44, 45. But putting the late date of these medals out of the question, it would be most unsafe to attach so much importance to anything found on coins. It is true that ancient nations were more in the

Fig. 40.

habit of depicting objects of art from things round about themselves than we are, but on the other hand the lyre had no doubt become established as a common ornament. It has been well remarked that should the statue of Handel, now in Westminster Abbey, survive all around it, and be the happy discovery of remote antiquaries, they will certainly believe that our great composer played on, and wrote for, the *lyre*, because he holds one in his hands. And should it also happen to be known that he actually did include a part for a theorbo, or arch-lute, in one of his works, the supposed fact will be considered firmly established.

We have now given an account of the stringed instruments mentioned in the Bible, and although opinions are still very conflicting as to their exact

Fig. 41.

nature, it is hoped a strong probability has been established that (1) the *kinnor* was a portable lyre; (2) the *nebel*, a harp of moderate size, but portable; (3) the *nebel-azor*, a ten-stringed *nebel*; (4) the *sabeca*, a triangular harp; (5) the *psanterin*, a psaltery or a dulcimer; (6) the *kithros*, a more fully developed lyre.

Before, however, leaving this division of our subject it seems necessary to say a few words on

several expressions used in the headings of the
Psalms and elsewhere, some of which are thought
by learned writers to contain definite directions as
to the stringed-instrument to be used, or to the
method of its tuning, &c.; in any case, they are

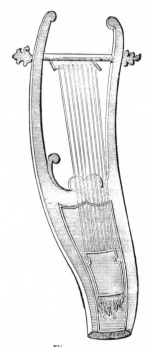

Fig. 42.

now generally considered to have some reference
to the musical accompaniment.*

Alamoth, one of these obscure words, occurs in
the title of Ps. xlvii., and also in Ps. lxviii. 25.
But as it is met with in the next quotation, in

* See Supplementary Note (1), to this Chapter.

juxtaposition with *sheminith*, it will be convenient to consider them together. " So the singers, Heman, Asaph, and Ethan, were appointed to sound with cymbals of brass ; and Zechariah, and Aziel, and Shemiramoth, and Jehiel, and Unni, and Eliab, and Maaseiah, and Benaiah, with psalteries on Alamoth; and Mattithiah, and Elipheleh, and Mikneiah, and Obed-edom, and Jeiel, and Azaziah, with harps on the Sheminith to excel " (1 Chron. xv. 19-21). Thus we see whilst some were set aside as players of cymbals, others were to play with *nebels on alamoth*, and others with *kinnors on the sheminith*.

Fig. 43.   Fig. 44.   Fig. 45.

Alamoth may mean " hidden things," or " things pertaining to youths " or " virgins." The first is adopted by St. Augustine, who applies it to the mysteries of the Gospel. But many authors, adopting the last meanings, have considered *alamoth* to mean songs for boys or virgins, or, in fact, for treble voices. But Dr. Jebb, in his learned dissertation on this word,* points out that the signification of " hidden things," or " mysteries," is inapplicable to its appearance in Ps. lxviii. 25 : " First go the *sharim* (singers), then follow the *neginim* (players);

* *A Literal Translation of the Psalms.* (Longmans, 1846 ; 2 vols.)

in the midst are the *alamoth*," where our version renders it "the damsels playing with timbrels." There is also one more reason why "virgins" or "boys" should not necessarily be implied in the term, namely, from a consideration of the passage above quoted (1 Chron. xv. 19-21), where the names of *men* are given as players on *nebels on alamoth*. It may, however, mean of a treble or high pitch, and it has been explained "vox clara et acuta quasi virginum"; but if this explanation refers to the *nebel* with which *alamoth* is associated, it will make *nebel* appear to be of a higher pitch than the *kinnor* which is associated with *sheminith*. This is a conclusion to which we should very unwillingly be driven; because the *kinnor* is the more ancient of the two, being (as has before been stated) the only stringed instrument mentioned in the Pentateuch, while the *nebel* is not named till we reach 1 Sam. x. 5; and, moreover, the *kinnor*, as being carried about hither and thither in the wanderings of the early tribes, must necessarily have been light and portable. If the *nebel* were of a pitch much higher than that of the *kinnor*, the *kinnor* must have been considerably larger to have made a suitable bass to it. Is it likely that a nation would succeed in carrying into captivity and preserving large harps? Yet the Israelites hung their *kinnors* in the willow branches which shadowed Babylon's waters. No; the *kinnor* was smaller than the *nebel*. Of course it may be urged that the *nebel*, even if a larger instrument than the *kinnor*, might have had so great an upward compass as to enable the performer on it to play above the pitch of the *kinnor*. But if this were the case, why should *sheminith* be associated with *kinnor*?

It is to this relation between *sheminith* and *alamoth* that we must look for the meaning of the latter, and as *sheminith* signifies " eighth," it is certainly fair to assume that *alamoth*, when connected with *nebel*, suggested also some numerical value, even if all traces of its precise meaning are now lost.

The exact application of the expression " on the eighth " *(sheminith)* with reference to *kinnors* is most difficult, or rather impossible to determine. The following seem to be the most important conjectures which have been hazarded—namely, that it refers (1) to the pitch of an octave; or (2) to the name of a scale or tune; or (3) to the number of strings on the instrument. As to the first of these, it must be admitted that it is ingenious, but a little consideration will show that there are serious objections to its acceptation. For although it is true that the octave is not only one of the best known intervals in music, as being the distance between the singing-pitch of men and women, but also the most important naturally, being produced by the simplest ratio of vibrations 1 : 2, yet the name " octave" could only be given to it by those who possessed a scale in which eight steps led from a note to its octave. Such a sound-ladder is of comparatively modern origin. The Greeks called the interval of an octave *diapason* (διὰ πασῶν) ; the position of an octave on a string *mese* (μέση), that is, "middle," because half the length of any string will produce the octave above the sound of the whole length ; and two sounds forming an octave they called, as to their relation to each other, *antiphonoi* (ἀντίφωνοι), as being " over against " or " responsive to " each other. But their scale consisted of a series of tetrachords, or groups of four notes in succession, some overlapping, that is, having one note common to two ; others being disjunct.

It is true that the Ambrosian chant, in the fourth century, and, two centuries later, the Gregorian modes, were to a certain extent limited in more than one way by the octave, but at the same time it was always attempted by teachers of music to graft the new on to the old system, although the former had indeed departed vastly from the principles of the latter.   Thus it will be found that a knowledge of ecclesiastical modes, and of the Greek tetrachords and harmonic ratios, formed the material of music-lore until the Guidonian system of hexachords became established in the eleventh century.   This system held its own for five or six centuries ;   in fact, its system of nomenclature seems to have been retained long after modern key-tonality was firmly settled.   It may then be safely said that " on the eighth " would not have directed the Levites to play in octaves.

As to the second explanation of *sheminith* which has been mentioned—namely, that it referred to an eighth " mode " or scale—all that need be said is, that even if the Hebrews did use various modes known by their numbers, there seems to be no reason for giving general directions that such and such men should play on *nebels* in one particular key, and other men on *kinnors* in some other key ; because if these instruments were always used and intended to be used in particular definite keys, why was it necessary to specify in which key ? The fact would be known.   But, on the other hand, if these instruments were capable of being tuned to many keys (as certainly was the case), why give command to certain Levites to play upon them only in one key? To believe that the expression refers to a special melody is equally impossible, as nothing could be more absurd than to suppose that such skilled musicians were set apart to play one tune. It might be so for one ceremony, but the close of chap. xvi. (1 Chron.) distinctly intimates that these Levites were chosen to be before the ark " continually," and those were chosen " who were expressed by name to give thanks to the Lord, because his mercy endureth for ever."

If " on the eighth " or " the eighth " refers to the number of the strings of the *kinnor*, we must be led to the interesting and natural conclusion, that these *nebels* and *kinnors* were used at different times, or at the will of different players, with various numbers of strings, and that the object was to procure uniformity in this respect.*

Gittith or *Ha-Gittith*, appears over Psalms viii., lxxxi., and lxxxiv. As being derived from a root signifying " wine-press," it has been translated in the Septuagint by ληνοί, and Vulgate by *torcularia*, both meaning " wine-presses," and some have thought it shows that the psalm is a vintage-song, or to be sung to some well-known vintage-song tune. But the word is also connected with " Gath," and it may have been an instrument brought from the city of Gath.†

---

* See next page and also Supplementary Note (2), to this Chapter.

† Probably tune-titles are also given in *Al-taschith* (Pss. 57-59, 75), *Jonath* (Ps. 56), *Muth-labben* (Ps. 9), and *Shushan* or *Shoshannim* (Pss. 45, 60, 69, 80). *Michtam* (Pss. 16, 56-60), and *Shiggaion* (Ps. 7), denote poems of a regular or irregular structure respectively. Songs of " degrees " or " going up " (Pss. 120-134) were for the use of pilgrims. For *Maschil* and *Mahalath* see p. 112, and for *Nehiloth* or *Nechiloth* p. 102.—(Ed.)

Aijeleth-shahar or *Aijeleth-he-shahar*, which occurs in Ps. xxii., signifies "hind of the morning," "dawn of day," or "morning twilight," supposed by many commentators to be the first line of words of a well-recognized tune to which this Psalm was to be sung; just as the Germans now call their chorales by the first line of the original words, even when other sets of words are adapted to them, as in the well-known instances, "O Haupt voll Blut und Wunden," "In allen meinen Thaten."

Alluding to the three words *Alamoth, Aijeleth,* and *Gittith,* Dr. Jebb contributes the following suggestion:—"It is to be observed that there are three Levitical cities, whose names resemble three designations in the titles [of the Psalms], *Alemeth, Aijelon,* and *Gath-Rimmon.* What is there, then, to hinder us from supposing that the designation *Alamoth* may mean harps that were constructed or improved by some Levite of *Alemeth;* that *Aijeleth-he-shahar* means a harp of *Aijelon;* and *Gittith,* one of Gath; just as we now speak of a German flute or a Cremona violin?"—*(Literal Translation of the Psalms. Dissertations.)*

Neginoth, in the singular *neginah,* occurs over several Psalms: as the root from which it is derived signifies "to strike a chord" (much the same as *psallere*), it probably is the collective term for stringed instruments. It is often joined with *kinnor,* though not with *nebel.* But if not joined with *kinnor* it often refers to that instrument, as, for example:—"And Saul's servants said unto him . . . Let our lord now command thy servants . . . to seek out a man, who is a cunning *player* [lit. striker] on an harp (*kinnor*). . . . And Saul said unto his servants, Provide me now a man that can *play* well, and bring him to me. Then answered one of the servants, and said, Behold, I have seen a son of Jesse the Bethlehemite, that is cunning *in playing*," &c. (1 Sam. xvi. 15-18; see also xviii. 10, and elsewhere). Dr. Jebb says *neginoth, sheminith,* and *kinnor* all refer to the same instrument: the first, to the mode of playing it; the second, to its compass; the last is its specific designation.

Shushan may mean " change," or more commonly " lily"; the latter, if it contains a musical reference, can only refer to the shape of an instrument—some have thought to cymbals, as being generally circular, with a deep central indentation. But it would be more applicable to the elegant outline of some of the lyres as shown in classical sculptures—such, for instance, as that in the celebrated " Apollo citharoedos." But it also may have a numerical meaning, suggesting the number " six." It is often joined with the word *eduth,* which signified " testimony " ; hence *shushan eduth* has been translated by Schleusner (quoted by Dr. Jebb) " the hexachord of testimony "—a highly poetical rendering, doubtless, but one which does not convey much definite information. As it is recorded in 1 Chron. xvi. 37-42 that part of the Levitical choir was stationed at Gibeon, where the tabernacle was pitched, and another part—the company of Asaph —at Jerusalem, to do honour to the ark of the testimony, it is possible that the *shushan eduth* meant the harp of six strings played at the latter, its distinctive name being retained after the junction of the two choral divisions.

Higgaion, translated in the Septuagint ᾠδή, appears in the Bible version of Ps. ix. 16—

" The Lord is known by the judgment which he executeth: the wicked is snared in the work of his own hands. Higgaion. Selah." The marginal note translates Higgaion as a "meditation." As the root of the word suggests " meditation," or " murmuring," and as it is used in Lam. iii. 62 of the murmurings of malicious enemies, the term can hardly be considered as a musical direction. But on the other hand it occurs in Ps. xcii. 3, in such an association as to render a musical reference almost necessary:—" Upon an instrument of ten strings, and upon the psaltery; upon the harp with a *solemn sound*," or, as the margin has it, more correctly, "upon the *higgaion* (solemn sound) with the harp." The Prayer-book version, it will be remembered, here reads " upon a *loud instrument*." It may possibly allude to a solemn and deep-toned performance on harps, which was found conducive to private meditation. Its conjunction with *Selah* makes this explanation the more probable.

The term *Selah*, which occurs three times in the Book of Habakkuk, and no less than seventy-one times in the Psalms, has been variously interpreted as indicating (1) a pause; (2) repetition (like *Da Capo*); (3) the end of a strophe; (4) a playing with full power (*fortissimo*); (5) a bending of the body, an obeisance; (6) a short recurring symphony (a *ritornello*). Of all these the last seems the most probable. In a lecture on the subject, given by Sir F. Ouseley, a Psalm was sung into which such *ritornelli* on stringed instruments and trumpets were introduced at every occurrence of the word *Selah*. The effect was considered imposing and devotional. The fact that twenty-eight of the thirty-nine Psalms in which this word occurs have musical superscriptions seems to compel belief that it was a direction to the musical performers.*

Minnim, which is derived from a root signifying "divided out," hence "a graded arrangement of strings," seems on all sides to be allowed to be a poetical allusion to stringed instruments generally, and is so translated in the last Psalm:—"Praise him with *stringed instruments* and organs." The word also occurs in Ps. xlv. 8, which would be better rendered thus: "Out of the ivory palaces the stringed instruments have made thee glad."

In conclusion, it may be said with regret that our information on the subject of Hebrew stringed-instruments is very scanty, so scanty as to warn us against entering into elaborate arguments on the exact shape and stringing in any particular case. The *kinnor* and the *nebel* appear to have been the only instruments of this class anciently consecrated to sacred uses, but there is no reason for doubting that other kinds became known to the Hebrews— such as the *nebel-azor*—and were included by them under the ancient names so intimately bound up with their religious worship. Minute details cannot be expected when the search is among occasional hints or allusions, which are in themselves accidental and not intended for the special information of the reader. We have reason to congratulate ourselves that modern writers have learned to distrust a vast amount of statements made by certain writers of the three or perhaps four last centuries. Some, who were for a long period held in much esteem (Kircher, for example), seem to have drawn largely upon their imagination when describing ancient musical instruments, and to have

* See Supplementary Note (3), to this Chapter.

thought that the best argument in favour of any
supposititious form of an instrument was to give a
good wood-cut of it!

The gradual development of stringed instruments
into various species is a subject of so great interest,
that a Plate is here appended giving the outline of
the more important of each group, starting from
the primitive hunting-bow, the playful twanging of
the strings of which in idle moments most probably
led to the construction of all musical instruments
of this class. This suggestion is painfully unpoetical,
and cannot for one moment hold its own, as far
as romance goes, against the pretty stories as to
the origin of such instruments handed down from
remote times amongst nearly every great race of
mankind. But it is, nevertheless, practically true;
and moreover its truth is not overthrown by the
fact that several species may occasionally be
merged into one another, or from time to time have
over-lapped in their growth. Of the evolutionary
series depicted on page 85, (a) is a hunting-bow, the
string of which is at such a tension that it would
emit a musical sound on being plucked; (b) shows
a primitive harp, formed by placing other strings
in a bow, parallel to the longest. Here, however,
is shown also the great improvement of a hollow
body or resonance-box for increasing the power of
the sounds—a discovery perhaps accidentally made
by placing a bow with several strings on a hollow
floor or empty inverted tub. (c) represents the outline
of the ancient instrument now used by the negroes,
and called a *nanga;* it consists of a primitive bow-
shaped body formed of a more extended arc than
its predecessor, probably on account of its greater
convenience for general use and for its portability.

It is distinctly the link between the harp (*b*) and the lute or guitar (*d*), known in Egypt perhaps as the *nefer*, and having counterparts in nearly every nation, civilised or savage, on the globe. The thin

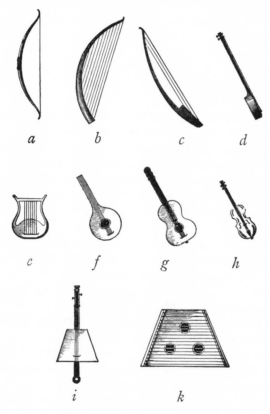

Suggested order of evolution.

upper portion of the body of the harp, made somewhat straighter in the *nanga* (*c*), has now become in the *nefer* (*d*) a veritable neck, and available as a

finger-board.   But again it must have been found
at a very early period, that if the two sides of a
bow are drawn very closely together by a rigid
material, as shown at (e), strings can be drawn at
right-angles to those in the primitive harp ;   thus
would the first lyre be formed, the circular base being
formed into a resonance-box.   When once, however,
the theory of a resonance-box was understood, the
existence of a *lute* (*f*) having a much larger
resonance-box than a lyre and a much shorter neck
than a *nefer*, became a mere matter of time.   The
transition from (*f*) to (*g*), that is from a lute to a
guitar, is so natural as to call for no remark ; the
indentations in the sides of the guitar, primarily
intended to make it lie comfortably on one leg of
the player, seem to have suggested the indentations
in the side of the violin family (*h*), so necessary for
the free movement of the bow.   At (*i*) there will be
seen an early fiddle, the Asiatic *rebab*, afterwards the
rebec, or three-stringed viol of Europe, in which the
absence of deep curved indentations is noticeable;
also, the shape of the resonance-box is interesting
as suggesting that when strings stretched over
a resonance-box were hit with hammers the
uselessness of the neck would be apparent ; such a
box, deprived of its head and tail, would form the
body of a dulcimer, as at (*k*).   When the hammers
of a dulcimer are connected with levers termed
" keys " we call it a pianoforte.*

It will be well to say at once that the above
sketch of the development of musical instruments
is not meant to be *chronologically* true : it is merely
intended to illustrate the remarkable correlation of
all stringed-instruments, ancient and modern.   The

* See Supplementary Note (4), to this Chapter.

use of a *bow* as a means of exciting vibrations of strings is in itself a most interesting fact, and suggests that the rubbing of one simple bow against another may have led to its discovery. Certainly bows are of great antiquity, many savage nations having instruments constructed like a *nefer* (*d*), but played with a bow. A glance at the same series will show how important a part of the growth of musical stringed-instruments is due to the resonance-box. In its early state it was merely formed by stretching a membrane of skin (commonly snake-skin) across a rounded open piece of wood or half a dried gourd. In its more elaborate form it was adjusted to the requirements of the compass of sounds to be produced by the strings, to their thickness, tension, and position; also by carefully selecting the finest specimens of wood for use, by giving consideration to its weight, closeness of fibre, &c., and finally, by determining the best *model* or " shape of the resonance-box." By innumerable experiments in such things, extending perhaps over thousands of years, we are at last in possession of an almost ideal type of violin, as turned out by the great Italian masters (Stradivarius in particular), who have so perfected the construction of this instrument with relation to its requirements, that the most skilful of modern workmen can make no better effort than to imitate their models, without indulging in a hope of ever surpassing them in general excellence.

The most primitive material used for strings was probably twisted grass; next in time, the guts of animals; lastly, wire or silk. Stringed-instruments closely allied to two or more of the family-types already depicted on page 85 are both numerous and

interesting. The *harp-lute*, a favourite instrument
at the close of the 18th century, good specimens of
which may often even now be found in the shops
of instrument-makers, possessed characteristics of
both harp and lute, having certain strings passing
over a fretted finger-board, while others were open
at the back. In the harpsichord, keys acted on
little *plectra* which plucked the strings; what the
ancient lyrists were compelled to do with their
fingers assisted by a plectrum, is here done by the
leverage of keys. In the pianoforte the hammers
are no longer left in the hands of the player, but
are also placed under the control of levers. The
old German *Streich-zither* was a link between the
guitar and fiddle; it was, as its name implies, a
bowed-guitar. A similar transition is suggested
by the old Italian *viola-lyra** (lyra-viol), once a
favourite instrument in this country.† This
transition is also implied by the fact that all
early viols had frets like a lute or guitar; the
frets were still in use when the instrument was
called a *violin* and no longer a *viol*.‡ Nor have
efforts been wanting to combine the effects
of keys and bows; several instruments have
from time to time been made in shape like a
pianoforte, but containing catgut strings, "bowed"
by a rotating resined wheel against which the action
of the keys forced the strings. The modern *zither*
combines the use of the plectrum of the ancient
lyrist with the flat resonance-box and wire strings

---

* See *Les Instruments à archet*, by Antoine Vidal. (Paris, 1876.)

† See *History of the Violin*, by Sandys and Forster. (London, 1864.)

‡ See Playford's *Introduction to the Skill of Music*, where instructions are
given for playing on this "cheerful and sprightly instrument . . . .
much practised of late." (14th edition, 1700.)

of the dulcimer. It has also certain strings over frets, thus possessing something in common with the lute family.

It will plainly be seen from what has been said that there are probably but few original progenitors —perhaps, indeed, only one—of the very large number of stringed-instruments now in existence.*

SUPPLEMENTARY NOTES.

(1.) In dealing with the difficult question of the Hebrew expressions used in the titles to the Psalms and elsewhere, the Rev. F. L. Cohen, who is well versed in the music of his race, when reading a paper before the Musical Association on the ancient musical traditions of the Synagogue, stated that in his opinion such words as *Gittith, Aijeleth, Jonath, Shushan, Alamoth,* refer to the "modes" or forms of chants to be used. These titles were added at a later date than the composition of the poems, and the vowels (in the shape of "points") were not inserted till the 7th century A.D. Hence he would read the words as *Gittith, Aiolith, Javanith, Susan, Elamith,* and they would mean the *Gathite, Æolian, Ionian, Susian,* and *Elamite* modes, corresponding to and paralleled by the geographical titles of the Greek modes. It is well known that in later times the teachers of the Temple music were principally Greeks. Professor Cheyne, in the *Encyclopædia Biblica* (*s.v.* Psalms, §26), offers another explanation of these Hebrew expressions. He considers that they are generally corruptions of the names of clans or guilds; thus *Alamoth* means "of Salmath" or the Salmæans, a division of the Temple singers, and *Sheminith,* according to him, stands for "of the Ethanim" or Nethinim, a well-known body of Temple servants. (*See,* however, the following note.)

(2.) With regard to *Alamoth* and *Sheminith,* when applied to the *nebel* and *kinnor* respectively, the ordinary

* See list of books recently published on the Evolution of Musical Instruments (p. 12).

explanation, with a necessary qualification, seems to be correct. For *Alamoth*, while meaning maidens, or " those kept apart," was very probably the title of a school or company of trained female singers and dancers attached to the religious worship of the Jews. In Egypt at the present day the *Al'meh* is a highly cultivated singer and performer—a truly "learned woman " as the Arabic name now implies—far removed from the common low-caste dancing girls (*ghawazee*). In ancient Egypt a small bow-shaped harp (Fig. 26) was especially used by these female singers, and to it they chanted as the Jews did to the sound of the *nebel* (Amos vi. 5), the Hebrew instrument with which I have already identified it (Chapter ii., Supplementary Note 1). Amongst the Temple musicians, therefore, ·there were players on the *nebel* for accompanying the girl singers and on the *kinnor* for the men's voices : for *Sheminith* may well mean "the octave," since both in Egypt and Assyria a seven-note scale of diatonic form was recognised by the cultured musicians, the five-note scale (pentaphonic rather than pentatonic)—for which Engel claimed so extensive and exclusive a use—being relegated to the populace after having been derived from the older form. It will be noticed that this qualified interpretation of the words *Alamoth* and *Sheminith* does not express the pitch of the instruments (treble or bass), about which Dr. Stainer found so much difficulty, but merely states that the *nebel* was considered the better accompaniment for female voices, and the *kinnor* for those of men. Nor is there any reason why men should not have been set apart to accompany on their *nebels* the girl singers, notwithstanding the objection urged on page 76.

(3.) Baethgen and other commentators consider that *Selah* is an attempt on the part of Hebrew scribes to represent the Greek word *Psallé* (ψάλλε) meaning " play," derived from some Greek bandmaster and used as the direction for a musical interlude. I am, however, greatly indebted to the Rev. E. Capel Cure, who has made an especial study of the poetry and musical allusions of the Psalter, for the clearest and most convincing account of the actual use of the *Selah*. His explanation is as follows, the quotations being made from the Revised Version :—" To say that *Selah*—whatever its derivation—is a musical interlude throws no light on the difficult problem which such passages present as are to be found in Psalm lv., verses 7, 19: for here there seems little sense in orchestral interludes rushing in upon incomplete similes and unfinished sentences, reducing both to meaningless incoherence. Surely the introduction of music in these and similar passages cannot have been intended for idle interruption, but for a definite purpose, that is, for an illustration in sound of the words sung, in the same way as a picture would present an illustration in line and colour of the letterpress. Such a sound-picture at once delays and sustains the imagination, filling (in the first instance mentioned above) the ears and mind of the listeners with the fury and noise of the storm through which the frightened dove beats its way to a peaceful wilderness: the longer the storm of clapping hands and beating feet lasted (imitating the roll of thunder and hiss of hail), the more the pulse of the harp arpeggios (so singularly like the beat of the dove's wing) was heard, now lost in the turmoil of these mingled means of musical description and now, as the rushing wind and rain lulled and lessened, rising with a triumphal sense of final safety, the more meaning did this intrusion of picture-music carry into the words with which at length the choir enter ' I would haste me to a shelter from the stormy wind and tempest.' So also in the 19th verse of the same Psalm, ' God shall hear and answer them ': thus sing the choir ; and there is no need for the poet to say more, for the instruments with an impressive eloquence indicate the horror of the answer. As in the *Selah* the reed-pipes wail out the familar funeral dirge, all men know what God's answer is: and when the dirge is finished and silence reigns, the choir complete the sentence to which this significant interruption has given such subtle irony, ' God will answer . . . the men who have no changes ' with the change of Death. *Selah* then is always a musical interlude, but not always what is known to modern critics as ' pure music.' Where it separates stanzas, it may be mere sound appealing by the beauty of its melody or combination of instruments: more often it represents what we now call 'programme music,' and is consciously and deliberately descriptive of the text which it accompanies.

"Besides the Flight and Storm motive, which we ascribe to the harps and clapping hands and feet, and which may be found very effectively employed also in Psalm lxi. after the 4th verse, ' I will take refuge in the covert of thy wings. *Selah*,' and besides the Death motive (probably given out on the reed-pipes) which illustrates so many Psalms with its cruel suggestiveness (Ps. lii. 5 ; lvii. 3 ; lix. 5, 13 ; &c.), there are two other *Selahs* in constant use—the Sacrifice and War *Selahs*— both with trumpets, though probably with different sorts of trumpets.

"It is known that the sound of trumpets accompanied the ritual of the altar, a blare of silver trumpets blowing, as it were, the sacrificial smoke heavenwards: once the victim was consumed the offertory music was silent. Here then is the explanation of the difficult words ' God is gone up with a shout, the Lord with the sound of a trumpet ' (Ps. xlvii. 5). The *Selah* preceding this verse was the sacrificial interlude of trumpets augmented with loud hallelujahs, which die away as the smoke grows thinner until, over the dying embers of the sacrifice, the Levites come in again to say that Jehovah, who had seemed to them to stoop from highest heaven to receive the gift, had returned once more to His lofty throne.

"The *Selah* in Psalm lxvi. 15, proves the poem to be a true service of the altar. ' I will offer bullocks with goats ' is sung, and straightway, in a pause which the priests fill with their trumpets, the bullocks and goats are really offered, after which the singers resume their song.

"The War motive is found picturesquely enough in Psalm lx. 4 and lxxvi. 3, and less certainly in Psalm l. 6. It would probably be given out on the *shophar*, the curved ram's horn, which had its own tremendous associations of alarm and terror (Exodus xix.). In Psalm xlix. there is a striking combination of motives : between verses 13 and 14 comes the Death *Selah* to emphasise the awful threat ' Death shall be their shepherd,' while the words of the later verse, 15, ' He shall receive me,' find their explanation in the Sacrificial *Selah*, trumpets declaring the favour of God on the living sacrifice of the worshipper's self and soul.

" With what eloquent effect the *Selah* could be used by one who was both artist and prophet may be seen in Habakkuk's hymn (Habakkuk, Ch. 3). Nowhere else in the Old Testament is anything so like our modern libretto to be found, where obviously the words are written with conscious regard to the effect and colour of the accompanying music.

" It is a most vivid word-picture of a tropical storm, which, however, depends on the orchestra for its fullest effect. The storm motive with its mimic thunder rushes in in the first *Selah* (verse 3) to explain how ' God came from Teman.' Always for the Israelite the Creator was behind His creation, but here His presence is audible. The music makes its own picture of heavy thunder-clouds, which envelop Mount Teman and come sweeping upward from the western horizon. Soon, however, words are introduced to give a clear description of the path and progress of the devastating storm, the wild melody being sustained and reinforced by a restless *agitato* of the string accompaniment. In effective contrast to this the composer provides a double opportunity for new orchestral colour in two other *Selahs*, intended not merely to relieve the ear, but, as it were, to illuminate and emblazon the truths which he wished to enforce. God's power, as exhibited in the rush of wind and roll of thunder, is the measure alike of His unbroken word and His awful justice. 'The oaths to the tribes were a sure word' (verse 9)—at once the strings are hushed before a blast of trumpets, carrying with it the solemn associations of the Sacrifice and all it implied of God's covenant of protection. But if there is mercy, there is also judgment; and the terrible vision of the battlefield, where the sweeping scimitar has exposed the very bones of the severed neck, receives a thrilling intensification, from the Death *Selah*, which immediately follows (verse 13).

" In this interpretation of the word *Selah*, it will be
seen that no excessive demand is made on the technique
or resources of primitive performers: but—while every
effect was produced by the simplest means — the
instrumentalists of the Temple did for the singers what
the artist does when he adds colour to the outline : in
fact, so much do some of the Psalms depend upon their
instrumental performance, that many of the phrases are
only intelligible with the due understanding of their
Selahs; while in all cases where the *Selah* is not a mere
symphony between stanzas, the interludes deepen the
glowing intensity of the words as much as Wagner's
music glorifies his libretti."

(4.) The origin of our present forms of musical
instruments is a subject of great interest, and reference
should be made to Mr. H. Balfour's *Natural History of
the Musical Bow* (Clarendon Press, 1899) and the other
recent works mentioned on page 12. As to Dr. Stainer's
statements it may be observed that the emanation of the
lyre from a closely bent hunting bow is hardly likely : it
is more probable that it had an independent origin, and
began with the tortoise-shell of popular story or some
other receptacle across which strings were stretched, a
form still found among some primitive African tribes and
enshrined in the psalteries and dulcimers of Asia and
Europe. To the tortoise-shell, extensions in the shape of
two arms were added, united by a cross-bar, which
permitted the use of longer strings. The *koto* or Japanese
psaltery is said by tradition to have been first constructed
out of a series of hunting-bows placed side by side, and
that later on they were merged into the one long sounding
body across which the strings are drawn. It appears
altogether unreasonable to suppose that the psaltery and
dulcimer form was derived from the *rebab* or an instrument
with a neck, as the author would suggest. The incurvations
to which we are accustomed in the sides of the modern
violin and guitar have their counterpart in a sculpture
found in the ruins of the Hittite palace of Eyuk near
Sinope, and dated about the year 1,000 B.C. (Plate III.).

PART II.

WIND INSTRUMENTS.

CHAPTER V.

KHALIL OR HALIL; MACHOL; MAHALATH.

THE universal usage of musical instruments of this class renders it difficult to reduce an account of them to reasonable limits. It will be well to state at once that in all probability the word *pipe*—the αὐλός of the Greeks, the *tibia* of the Romans—included two important divisions of modern instruments: namely, *reed* instruments, such as the oboe or clarinet; and simple *flue* pipes, such as the flute. That this must have been the case is evident from the fact that while there is unquestionable evidence that many ancient instruments had reeds, no special name is set apart for them as opposed to open tubes without reeds. The very existence of the word γλωσσόκομον (tongue-box)* shows that the player was accustomed to carry his tongues or reeds separately

---

* This word, it will be remembered, is used in St. John xii. 6 and xiii. 29, where it is translated *bag;* but it is quite possible that Judas Iscariot carried the money in a "reed-box," as implied by the Greek text.

from his instrument, just as our modern oboists and clarinetists do. It must also be borne in mind that both oboe and clarinet are children of one parent, and did not become distinct classes until the early part of the 18th century, the parent name being *chalumeau*, from the Latin *calamus*, Greek κάλαμος, a cane or reed. But when *chalumeau* is translated "a reed-pipe," it must not be forgotten that the term is applied to the material of which the pipe is made (a cane), and not, as we always apply the term now, to a pipe containing a reed or tongue. Hence it will be seen that we are no nearer the discovery of distinctive names for these two classes of instruments, even when their parent stock is found. It may be worth mentioning that the real difference between an oboe and a clarinet is that the former has a double tongue which vibrates, the latter a single tongue.*

The derivations of some of the ancient names of flutes are very interesting: *khalil* or *halil*, from a root signifying "pierced" or "bored"; *tibia* (Lat.), from the fact that it was often made of a shinbone; *aulos* (αὐλός), from the root ἄω, αὔω, "to blow," exactly corresponding to our *flute*, from the Lat. *flo*, "to blow," as also flageolet, from *flatus*; *calamus* (κάλαμος), *chalumeau*, from the material, just as the Arabian flute is called *nay*, "a reed," of which the Arabs have as many as ten varieties. There was also a small Phœnician flute called *gingra* (γίγγρα), which is probably connected with Sanskrit *grî*, "to sound."

Was the *khalil* a flute or oboe? Probably the latter. There is evidence from many sources that the Hebrews had oboes (*see* Lightfoot, who

---

* See Supplementary Note (1), to this Chapter.

speaks, in his *Temple Service*,* of oboes being used once in each month), and there seems to be no good reason for believing that they had a distinctive term for them. Jahn thinks it probable that they were very similar to the *zamr* of the Arabs, of which there are three kinds, not differing essentially from each other, but only in size and pitch, the largest being called *zamr-al-kébyr ;* the middle sized, as being most commonly used, *zamr ;* and the smallest *zamr-el-soghayr.* Fig. 46 shows two of these.

It is probably known to the reader that large and small oboes have always existed, and are in

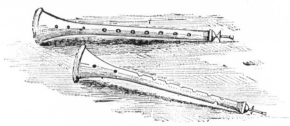

Fig. 46.

use at the present day. Two sorts are used in the score of Bach's Passion Music (according to St. Matthew), called respectively *oboe d'amore* (the love oboe), and *oboe da caccia* (hunting-oboe) ; the part of the former, the smaller of the two and possessing a soft delicate tone, can, with a transposition of the lower notes, be played on the common oboe ; that of the latter on the tenor oboe, commonly, but very improperly, termed *corno-inglese*, or the English horn.

---

* In the later Temple Services not less than two and not more than twelve pipes were allowed. See Edersheim *The Temple . . . at the time of Jesus Christ*, Chapter iii.

Of the pipes without reeds, like our flutes, there always have been two kinds : one played by blowing in one end, hence held straight in front of the performer; the other played by blowing in a hole in the side, hence held sideways. The former was ultimately called the *flûte à bec*, that is, the flute with a beak ; the latter, *flauto traverso*, that is, the flute played crossways.* Fig. 47 is an illustration of a *flûte à bec* which was brought from Egypt. It belonged to a Mahometan pilgrim, who vowed that he valued it more than anything he owned, but he was very willing to part with it at the sight of a

Fig. 47.

Fig. 48.

small sum of money. It is of cane, and is rudely ornamented with simple patterns. It seems closely allied to the *souffarah* of the Arabs. The next illustration (Fig. 48) shows an ancient Egyptian reed-flute—*piffero di canna* as it is labelled—in the museum at Florence. It was held obliquely and blown across the upper open end.

These instruments seem, judging from the specimens found in Egyptian sculpture or frescoes, to have been of various lengths, sometimes far exceeding the size of the flute commonly used in

* See Supplementary Note (2), to this Chapter.

our orchestras. This goes to prove that this nation was wise enough to make use of a family of flutes, just as we use a family of viols. And there are many musicians who think that we lose much by thus excluding flutes of deeper tone. Within the last few years concerts have been given in London at which quartets were played by four flutes—treble, alto, tenor, and bass.

Fig. 49 represents an Egyptian playing on one of these oblique flutes. The attitude will not strike a modern flautist as being either comfortable or convenient, but there is no accounting for the conventionalities of art. One thing the Ancients lacked which has been of inestimable benefit to us,

Fig. 49.

the use of keys—that is, a simple system of leverage by which holes in the instrument quite out of reach of the length of the ordinary human five fingers can be brought completely under control, and can be closed or opened without any great disturbance of the position of the hand.* The thumb, which could not possibly close a hole at the top of the instrument in former times, is now able to do so. Thus both the compass of the

* See, however, Supplementary Note (3), to this Chapter.

instrument and the ease with which it can be manipulated have been largely increased. It must not be supposed that such improvements have been rapidly created. They are mainly of the last century, invented by Gordon, perfected by the ingenious Boehm.

It is remarkable that the oblique flute, as shown in the Egyptian drawing (Fig. 49) is not to be found on any Assyrian or Chaldean monuments. If then the Jews used it, they must have adopted it from Egypt, which is also acknowledged to be the source from whence the Greeks obtained it.

Two ancient Greek *auloi* or pipes, found in a tomb, are preserved in the British Museum. Their great age renders the wood from which they are made extremely frail, and any rough usage would probably reduce them to dust.

They were played with reeds, probably of the oboe or double kind : but Fétis is of opinion that they had single tongues, like our clarinet, only he is inclined to think that the tongue was of metal, not of wood, because in a certain account given of a trial of musical skill, one player was unable to compete because the reed of his instrument was *bent*. But it is probably assuming too much to say that such an accident could not have happened to a wooden tongue, and that, therefore, brass was the material of which it was made. One thing, however, is certain, and that is, that in the earliest forms of *calamus* the reed would naturally be of cane, because it would be simply formed by an incision in the surface of the cane itself, similar to that made by boys in a piece of straw, when constructing that toy instrument dignified by pastoral poets by the name of " oaten pipe."

The *khalil* seems to have been used by the Jews on very similar occasions to those at which our ancient oboes played an important part, most often during seasons of pleasure, but sometimes also at funerals. Two pipes at least had to be played at the death of a wife. The pipers, it will be remembered, were bidden to "give place" by our Lord, when He said, "The maid is not dead, but sleepeth" (Matt. ix. 24). One common use of the *khalil* was as an amusement and recreation when walking or travelling. The solitary shepherd would cheerily pipe as he paced out his long hillside walks, and the path of the caravan could be traced by the shrill echoes ever and anon tossed from side to side as, at each new turn in its many windings, frowning rocks beat back the piercing sounds. Especially such was the case when thousands of persons were making those periodical journeys to Jerusalem, so rigidly prescribed by the law : " Ye shall have a song, as in the night when a holy solemnity is kept; and gladness of heart, as when one goeth with a pipe (*khalil*) to come into the mountain of the Lord, to the mighty One of Israel" (Isa. xxx. 29). The joy of the people when the cry " God save king Solomon ! " promised a peaceful and prosperous reign, was shown by their music: " The people piped with pipes, and rejoiced with great joy, so that the earth rent with the sound of them " (1 Kings i. 40). The *khalil* is not so often mentioned in connection with the outpouring of prophetic gifts as are instruments of the harp class ; but yet when Samuel was describing to Saul how he should meet a company of prophets on his way to Gilgal, he described them as " coming down from the high place with a psaltery (*nebel*), and a tabret (*toph*), and a pipe (*khalil*), and a harp (*kinnor*) before them" (1 Sam. x. 5). But these instruments were elsewhere to be met with than at the solemn processions of holy men, for the prophet Isaiah, in denouncing the drunkards who "rise up early in the morning to follow strong drink," describes their wine feasts as being enlivened by the sounds of the *nebel*, *kinnor*, *toph*, and *khalil* (Isa. v. 12). The prophet Jeremiah, in showing the utter desolation and destruction of Moab, is inspired to say, "I will cause to cease in Moab, saith the Lord, him that offereth in the high places, and him that burneth incense to his gods. Therefore mine heart shall sound for Moab *like pipes*, and mine heart shall sound *like pipes* for the men of Kir-heres. . . . There shall be lamentation generally upon all the house-tops of Moab, and in the streets thereof: for I have broken Moab like a vessel wherein is no pleasure, saith the Lord" (Jer. xlviii. 35, 36, 38). Could any words describe more touchingly than these the degradation and loss of moral life which should overtake Moab? That it should be wept over as one dead, piped over as a corpse!

There is no direct evidence as to whether the Hebrews used the *double* reed-pipe. It is quite certain they must have been aware of its existence, because it was known to Phœnicians, Assyrians, Egyptians, and Chaldees before it found its way into Greece. So common is it in Roman and Greek sculpture and pottery that all are familiar with its forms. The word *nechiloth* is understood by Jahn and Saalchütz to mean the double-pipe; but on the other hand, many others consider *nechiloth* to be

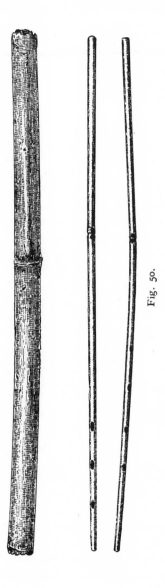

Fig. 50.

the collective term for wind instruments. Some
consider that *nekeb*, which is derived from a root

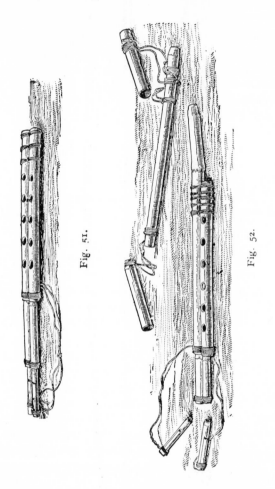

Fig. 51.

Fig. 52.

signifying " hollow," stands for the double-pipe;
but this word probably signifies the hollow place

in which a gem is set.* The two tubes forming the double-pipe were called oddly enough male and female, but more commonly right and left (*dextra* and *sinistra*). The former appellation no doubt refers to the fact that one tube produced a deep note, which served as a drone or bourdon, while on the other was played the tune. The difference in the pitch might easily have given rise to the comparison implied between the two names.

Two ancient Egyptian reed-pipes found in the tomb of the Lady Maket (*c.* 1100 B.C.), together with their case, are illustrated in Fig. 50 (page 103), and a description of them is given in the Supplementary Note 4 (p. 114).

Double-pipes, almost similar in their construction, are actually in use among the present inhabitants of Egypt. Two specimens are shown in Figs. 51 and 52. That in the latter illustration has three loose pieces, which may be added at pleasure to the " drone " tube of the instrument for the purpose of adjusting it to the key of the tune to be played. That in the former has two similarly constructed pipes, so that a simple melody may be performed in two parts, much in the same way as on the double-flageolet, which at one time was somewhat popular in England, though now rarely seen or heard. Both examples are of the simplest construction. The material of which they are made (including the mouth-pieces and tongues) is of river-reed, cut into lengths, which have to be inserted into each other before use. To prevent accidental loss, the separate parts are connected

---

* The close of Ezek. xxviii. 13 should therefore be " the workmanship of the jewels, and the setting of the stones " (*not* " of thy tabrets and of thy pipes ").

by common waxed cord.   These instruments are
called *arghool ;* they are furnished with single
beating reeds, and have distinguishing titles,
according to the length of the drone-tube.

Fig. 53.

Fig. 54.

In Fig. 53 the inequality in the length of the two
pipes is very apparent.   Fig. 54 shows that they
were sometimes used in Egyptian ceremonies of a
solemn character.   In Fig. 55 is shown the
capistrum, which Greeks and Romans wore to give

support to muscles of the cheeks and face whilst blowing. In modern orchestras we are perfectly content with the quantity of tone produced from our wind-instruments without the assistance of these head-bandages.

On the next page an Assyrian is shown with a double-pipe (Fig. 56). It is to be regretted that no details as to the construction of these instruments can be gleaned from the ancient bas-reliefs. No

Fig. 55.

attempt seems to have been made to mark even the position of the holes.

The use of the double-pipe by nations with whom the Jews had constant intercourse having been shown, nothing more can be said. The reader must form his own opinion as to the probability of its being rightly enrolled amongst Hebrew musical instruments. The quality of tone produced by these reed-pipes was probably very coarse and crude. Particular pains have been taken by modern instrument-makers to produce delicate-sounding oboes, clarinets, &c. And with regard to the open pipes and flutes of the Ancients, it should be borne in mind that it must have been most difficult to produce a series of sounds, either similar in timbre

Fig. 56.

or perfectly true in pitch, without the aid of keys. Up to the last century, certain holes in the then existing flutes had to be only partially covered by the fingers in order to produce certain notes in tune. We must learn from this, not to place much confidence in conclusions drawn from actual experiments on old pipes. Suppose, for instance, it were attempted to discover the series of scale-sounds of such an instrument by placing it in the hands of a modern performer. It would be impossible to say whether any noticeable variations from known forms of the scale ought to be attributed to the intentional design of the instrument itself, or to our loss of those traditions which influenced its use. But we may have to say something about the musical scales of the Ancients when speaking further on of the vocal music of the Hebrews.

MACHOL, OR MAHHOL.

This word is found in several passages of Holy Scripture associated with the *toph* or timbrel. In the Authorised Version it is rendered almost always by " dances " or " dancing " :—" And Miriam, the prophetess, the sister of Aaron, took a timbrel in her hand ; and all the women went out after her with timbrels and with dances " (Exod. xv. 20) ; and again, " Jephthah came to Mizpeh unto his house, and, behold, his daughter came out to meet him *with timbrels and with dances* " (Judges xi. 34). In thus rendering *machol*, our translators have simply followed the Septuagint, in which the corresponding expression is ἐν τυμπάνοις καὶ χοροῖς ; the same, too, in the Vulgate, " cum tympanis et choris." The German, like our own version, follows the Septuagint—" mit Pauken und Reigen," that is, " with drums and chain-dances," dances with linked hands. Although in modern German orchestral scores *Pauken* signifies " kettledrums," it

must not be supposed that more is here meant than
tambourines (timbrels). That dances took place on
these and many other occasions in which timbrels
were used there can be no doubt.   But may not
machol signify a small flute ? If so, the expression
with *toph* and *machol* would exactly correspond to
our old English *tabor* and *pipe*, to the sounds of
which instruments many a rustic dance was merrily
footed.   They are still the common accompaniment
of village festivities in many parts of Europe.   In
some of the Pyrenean districts may be seen gathered
on the green, round which their homesteads are
clustered, the gaily attired villagers dancing to the
sounds of a pipe which the seated musician plays
with his left hand, while with his right hand he
beats a sort of tambour, consisting of six strings
stretched across a resonance-box, which rests upon
his knees, or is held by his arm, taking the place
of the more usual drum.

The arguments in favour of the theory that
machol is a flute are founded on the fact that
many authors, amongst them Pfeifer, consider the
word itself to be derived from the same root as
khalil, signifying, as before mentioned, " bored
through "; and also that in the Syriac version the
word is translated by *rephaah*, which is the name
of a flute still to be found in Syria.   On the other
hand, some authors have traced *machol* to a root
khol, " to twist or turn round "; and, of course, if
this be a correct derivation, it would more naturally
signify a dance than a flute.   Saalchütz is of
opinion that it implies a combination of music,
poetry, and dancing, and is not the name of any
special musical instrument.   Much can be said in
favour of this view.   We have words in our own

language which have a very similar meaning: for
instance, *roundelay*, which may be taken as a song,
a dance, or a piece of poetry. Yet there seems to
be but little necessity for forcing such a mixed
meaning from the word *machol*. To say that on a
joyous occasion men or women went forth with
"pipe and timbrel," is enough to imply that they
danced; and therefore, if our translators would
have more properly rendered *machol* by a "pipe,"
they have none the less conveyed the real sense of
the context by rendering it "dancing." But by
assuming the former of these interpretations much
force is given to that beautiful passage in the Book
of Lamentations (v. 15): "The joy of our heart is
ceased; our pipe is turned into mourning." The
Psalmist in his joy uses just the converse of this
expression, in Ps. xxx. 11 : "Thou hast turned for
me my mourning into dancing *(machol)*; thou hast
put off my sackcloth, and girded me with gladness."
So does the prophet, joying over the restoration
of Israel (Jer. xxxi. 4 and 13). The only other
passage in which the Psalmist uses the word is in
Ps. cl. 4: "Praise him with the timbrel and
dance." It was the noise of the pipes *(macholoth)*
which Moses heard as he descended the holy
mount to find the people, whom Jehovah had but
just highly honoured by the giving of the Law,
dancing round a golden calf. We may, then, for
two reasons believe the *machol* to have been a flute
used specially for dancing: first, because it is
highly probable that an instrument was used in
conjunction with the timbrel; and next, because
such a supposition does not exclude the idea of
dancing, and in no case seems to do violence to
the text.

MAHALATH, OR MACHALATH.

A word allied both to *khalil* and *machol* occurs in the titles of two Psalms (liii. and lxxxviii.), the former being inscribed to the "chief musician upon Mahalath," the latter to the "chief musician upon Mahalath Leannoth." Each of these is called also a "Maschil," a title generally thought to designate a poem of a moral or typical import. "Sing ye a *maschil* with the understanding," sings the Psalmist in Ps. xlvii. 7. Many learned writers trace *mahalath* to the same root as *khalil* ("perforated," "bored"). If a musical direction, then, this word clearly points out the class of instruments which is to accompany the singers of the Psalm—namely, *khalil.* The addition *leannoth*, from the fact that it means "to answer," most probably is a special order for an antiphonal treatment.

SUPPLEMENTARY NOTES.

(1.) In deriving the oboe and the clarinet from a common parent the author probably meant that in their primitive form both of them were made of river reeds, for the principle of the double-beating reed (as used with the oboe) and that of the single-beating reed (as found on the clarinet) are quite distinct. The double-reed is probably the older of the two forms, at least in Europe and Asia, and was evolved from the simple method of pressing together the end of a hollow straw, as is still done by country children of our own day; but in the Western Hemisphere, if we may draw an inference from the reed-pipes constructed by the Indians living on the north-west coast of America, the single-beating form seems to have been the earlier: for *twin* single-reeds are still made there with a thin slip of wood between them, and it was probably by removing this partition that the double-reed was obtained. The distribution of the two kinds of reed is also very marked: in ancient Egypt, as well as in that of to-day, the characteristic type is the single-beating reed; in China and the Far East only the double-reed is prevalent.

(2.) The flutes or flue-pipes are more correctly grouped into the two classes: *(a)* vertical and *(b)* transverse. The vertical flute, of which the old Egyptian oblique flute and the present Arabian *nay* are examples, were sounded by forcing the breath across the open end of the tube, while the transverse flutes (with a closed end) are played by blowing across a hole pierced in the side as in their probable parents—the nose flutes.

Though the principle is practically the same in both cases, the two types are distinct: for although the vertical flute, with its offspring the whistle flute or *flûte-à-bec*, is generally distributed throughout both Hemispheres, the transverse flute was unknown in Europe until the 8th or 9th centuries of our era, having travelled gradually westward from eastern Asia and India. In the vertical flutes of the Chinese and of the North American Indians, the growth of the *flûte-à-bec*, with its well-formed mouthpiece, can be distinctly traced from the primitive tube blown across the end.

(3.) Recent discoveries have shown that the Greeks and Romans of classical times were not ignorant of devices for stopping additional holes on their reed-pipes, after the manner of keys. On *auloi* found at Pompeii small revolving rings of metal cover the holes that were not required for the mode or scale in which the music was set, and by turning the rings these holes could be brought into use, and those not needed silenced. On a reed-pipe found in the ruins of Pergamos, in Asia Minor (and now in the Archæological Institute at Berlin), a yet nearer approach is made to keyed mechanism: for metal sliders working in grooves cover the holes that are out of reach of the player's fingers, to each slider a metal shaft being attached whereby it can be drawn up or down by the performer, thus opening the hole or closing it at will. Keys, in the modern sense of the word, appear in the early part of the 16th century, as shown on the *phagotum* of Canon Afranio, of which a detailed description and illustrations are given in Theseo Ambrogio's *Introductio in Chaldaicam Linguam* (1539).

(4.) The double-pipes of the Ancients were played sometimes with double-beating reeds and sometimes with single reeds; and although the two pipes may have served at times as melody and drone, in the same way as the present Egyptian *arghool* and some of the Indian pipes are used, yet as a rule both tubes were furnished with finger-holes. An Egyptian double-pipe of slender reeds was discovered by Prof. Flinders Petrie, in 1890, amongst the relics of the tomb of the Lady Maket (*c.* 1100 B.C.), and is now deposited in the Royal Museum at Berlin, having been purchased for £73 (Fig. 50). The tubes are of almost the same length—17¾ inches; but one is pierced with four holes, the other with three. No reeds were found with them, but by using a single-beating reed of the *arghool* type, the following scales have been produced: On the left-hand or four-holed tube, E flat, G (slightly flat), A flat, B flat (slightly flat), and C flat; while on the right-hand tube the order was E flat, F, G, and A flat. On an *aulos* found at Akhmin (the Panopolis of older days) in 1888, eleven holes were noted, and when a facsimile of the original was sounded with a single-beating reed, it furnished a complete chromatic scale throughout the octave, with a possible enharmonic note included. In its original state the sounding reed of the instrument was hidden within a hollow bulb of rush or river-reed, as so often depicted in Etruscan art and still used in the bagpipe and other rustic pipes of the present day. Although this interesting specimen is pronounced by Egyptologists to be of the eighteenth Dynasty (*c.* 1500 B.C.), it is more reminiscent both in scale and structure of the much later instruments found at Pompeii.

CHAPTER VI.

WIND INSTRUMENTS (*continued*).—GHUGGAB,

OUGAB, OR UGAB.

HAVING spoken of the pipe, and of the possibility that the Hebrews knew of the double-pipe, we naturally come to those instruments which place a number of pipes under the control of the performer. At first it should be remarked that there is an essential difference between the *flûte à bec*, or flute with a beak, and the *flauto traverso*, which it was unnecessary to point out when these instruments were previously mentioned. It is this: in the former class, the performer has only to blow into the end, and the sound is produced by the air being led by the form of the interior against a sharp edge of wood termed the *upper lip*. In the *flauto traverso* (now the common flute), the player, by adjusting the form of his lips, has *himself* to force the air against the edge of one of the holes, which he thus temporarily makes into an *upper lip*. By comparing a penny whistle with the ordinary military fife this difference of their construction will be very apparent. In the former, a piece of wood placed in the mouth-piece guides the column of air to the opening, where it is compelled to pass the under lip (the lower edge of the opening), so as to strike against the upper lip; but in the latter nothing of the sort is provided, the player making his mouth the *under lip*, and, as before said, the side of the hole the upper lip. It is plain, therefore, that two classes of "manifold-pipes" can exist, the one corresponding to a collection of *flauti traversi*, the other to a collection of *flûtes à bec.**

Now, if we take any piece of a tube open at both ends, and blow against the sharp edge until a musical sound is produced, we are acting exactly on the same principle as does the player on the *flauto traverso*. And if now we place our hand so as to *close* the other end of the tube, the pitch will immediately fall to an octave lower than it was before, for physical reasons that need not here be entered into. In both cases, whether the tube be open or closed, we are producing the sound on the same principle.

A collection of tubes of different sizes stopped at one end, and blown into at the other as above described, forms the musical instrument known as Pan's-pipe, in the Greek *syrinx* (σῦριγξ), Latin *fistula;* whereas a collection of *flûtes à bec* of different sizes placed in a series of holes in a box, through which the air can be forced mechanically, constitutes what has for centuries been distinctively called the *organ*. This difference between these two instruments is of the more importance, because it is a commonly received notion that the *syrinx* is the parent of the organ. Unquestionably, as regards antiquity, the former instrument must be allowed to have priority, but this does

* See Supplementary Note (1), to this Chapter.

not necessarily prove any connection between the two.

From what has been said, it will be easily imagined that a Pan's-pipe blown by mechanical means would really be a very scientific instrument; but on the other hand, when *flûtes à bec* were once commonly used, it would not require any special ingenuity or invention to suggest that several should be placed in a row over a box, and be blown one after another from the same supply of wind. Of course, as each organ-pipe was only

Fig. 57.

required to give one sound, there would be no necessity for finger-holes being made in it. Again, it must very soon have been discovered that pipes containing *reeds* could as easily be made to speak over a wind-box as flue-pipes.

The universality of the Pan's-pipe is as remarkable as its antiquity. To find a nation where it is not in use is to find a remarkable exception. In an ancient Peruvian tomb a *syrinx* was discovered and acquired by General Paroissen. A plaster cast of this interesting relic was lent for exhibition at South Kensington Museum in 1872, by Professor Oakeley, of Edinburgh (Fig. 57).

The description of the original, as given in the catalogue, was as follows:—" It is made of a greenish stone, which is a species of talc. Four of its tubes have small lateral finger-holes, which, when closed, lower the pitch a semitone." The Inca Peruvians called the syrinx *huayrapuhura*. The British Museum possesses one of these, consisting of fourteen pipes. The example shown in Fig. 58 has been selected in order to show how little even savage nations have departed from the earliest known classical form of the instrument. It represents a *syrinx* from the island of Tanna, New Hebrides. All must be so familiar with the many representations of Pan playing his river-reed pipes, that it is quite unnecessary to give an illustration of one of them. It should be said, however, that the commonest number of reeds used among the Ancients was seven, but eight or nine or even more are occasionally found.

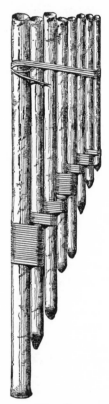

Fig. 58.

Was the *ugab* a *syrinx* or an organ ? As the former seems to have been the more ancient of the two, and as *ugab* is included in the very first allusion to musical instruments in the Bible, it would seem reasonable to say at once that it was a *syrinx*, especially as this instrument was, and is to this day, commonly met with in various parts of Asia. Yet it would indeed be strange if such an instrument were selected for use in Divine worship; and that the *ugab* was so used is proved beyond a doubt by its mention in Ps. cl.: "Praise him with the *minnim* and *ugab*." Its mention here in conjunction with the collective name for stringed instruments surely points to the fact of its being a more important instrument than a few river-reeds fixed together with wax. Let us not forget that we have but one and the same name for the single row of about fifty pipes, placed, perhaps, in a little room, and the mighty instrument of 5,000 pipes, occupying as much space as an ordinary dwelling-house and requiring the daily attention of a qualified workman to keep its marvellous complications properly adjusted. Each is an organ. May it not have been the case that the *ugab*, which in Gen. iv. 21 is mentioned as the simply-constructed *wind*-instrument, in contrast to the simple *stringed*-instrument, the *kinnor*, was a greatly inferior instrument to that which in Ps. cl. (before quoted) is thought worthy of association with a word which embraces all the stringed instruments?

Even if it be insisted that the first-mentioned *ugab* was nothing more than a *syrinx*, are we therefore forbidden to believe that the mere name might have been retained while the instrument itself was gradually undergoing such alterations and improvements as to render it in time a veritable organ? That men's minds have from the earliest times striven to find out in what way many pipes could be brought under the control of a single player, there are indubitable proofs. A passage in the Talmud,* describing an instrument called *magrepha,* which was said to be used in the Temple, is exceedingly interesting. The word *magrepha* signifies " a fork," and the instrument was so named because of the similarity of the outline of its upright pipes to the prongs of a fork. This organ, for it is entitled to the name, had a wind-chest containing ten holes, each communicating with ten pipes; it therefore was capable of producing 100 sounds. These were brought under the control of the player by means of a *clavier,* or key-board. Its tones were said to be audible at a very great distance.

Supposing that the whole of this account is apocryphal, it still shows that in the 2nd century such an instrument was not only considered *possible,* but believed, rightly or wrongly, actually to have existed at some previous period.

Let us now trace the various stages through which the organ has passed, while developing from what we should now consider a toy, to that noble instrument which makes our beautiful cathedrals and churches ring again with sweet sounds, and whose duty it is to guide and support the combined voices of many hundreds, or it may be thousands, of hearty hymn-singers.

Assuming that a series of wood or metal *flûtes à bec* had been constructed so as to give in succession the notes of a scale, and also that the wind-chest was pierced with holes to receive them, the first

---

* *Mishna,* Tr. Erachin., Chapter ii., sections 3, 5, 6. The same instrument is also referred to in other passages under the names *ardablis* and *hardules,* which seem to be attempted transliterations of *hydraulis,* the Greek title of the water-organ described in Supplementary Note (2), to this Chapter.

thing required by the player would be a contrivance
for allowing him to make any particular pipe speak
separately. As might be supposed, the simplest
method of doing this is to place little slips of wood
in such a position that they can either be pushed
under the foot of the pipe, and so stop the current
of air from passing into it, or be pulled out so
as to admit the air.

Fig. 59 exhibits this most simple piece of
mechanism, and very possibly shows what the
ugab might have been at some period of its
existence. A tube at the side of the wind-chest
points to the fact that the commonest bellows of
the period was considered capable of supplying the

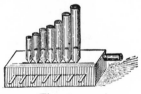

Fig. 59.

required current of air. The whole construction is
in a more advanced state in the instrument depicted
in Fig. 60. Not only are its pipes more numerous,
but it has bellows specially adapted to its
requirements. While one bellows is being
replenished, the other is still able to support the
sounds, so there is no awkward pause while the
instrument is taking breath.

In the next illustration (Fig. 61), which is from
a MS. Psalter of Eadwine, in the library of Trinity
College, Cambridge, the organ has begun to assume
a more dignified form. There is an attempt at an
ornamental case, and judging from the number of

blowers required, the music must have been rapid, or the sounds powerful.*

As soon as these instruments became large and not easily movable, the terms *positive* and *portative* organ came into existence—the former being an instrument which, owing to its size, had to

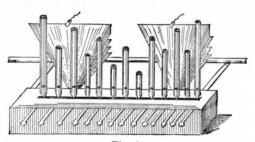

Fig. 60.

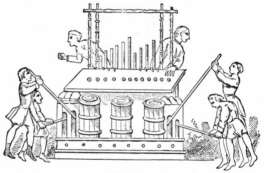

Fig. 61.

remain stationary; the latter, one that could be carried about. In the 16th century, these portable organs were called *regals*, the exact derivation of which is somewhat uncertain. They formed a very important element in ecclesiastical

---

* This is a representation of the *hydraulus* or water-organ   [ED.].

processions, as their cases were frequently elegantly decorated.   Fig. 62 on the next page shows a German *positive* organ of the 16th century, the shutters of which are also elaborately painted. This instrument has iron handles, by which it can be moved, but it is too large to have been of the *portative* class.   The bellows, which are behind it and so not seen in the figure, are very similar both in position and shape to those seen in Fig. 60.

In attempting to form some opinion as to the degree of excellence reached by builders of ancient (not mediæval) organs, it is very necessary to bear in mind that the principles on which instruments of this class are constructed have not undergone any radical change since the earliest times. Indeed, one of our huge modern organs exhibits an ingenious expansion of old ideas, rather than the invention of new.   Let us suppose, for example, that we have two rows of pipes (*i.e.*, two stops), one set of metal, the other of wood, standing in holes in the top of a box, which is supplied with air (under suitable compression) from a bellows. Only two problems present themselves: first, how is the player to make any particular pipe speak while its neighbours stand silent; next, how is the player to have power to play on whichever of the two sets of pipes he may wish.   When these questions are answered we shall have discovered the two important principles on which *all* organs have been and are constructed. The modern names for the two pieces of mechanism which bring about these results are, respectively, the *pallet* and the *slider*. In Fig. 59 is shown the simplest method of placing particular pipes under the player's control.   Slips are here moved in

Fig. 62.

and out from under the foot of the pipes. The utter impossibility of obtaining from such a system a rapid succession of sounds, or the simultaneous movement of several slips so as to produce a chord, will at once be evident. In modern organs there lies under the foot of each pipe, some little distance below it, a small flat piece of wood covered with leather, which is hinged at one end and kept in

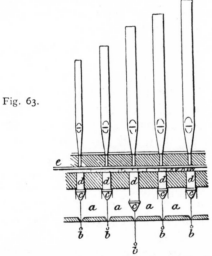

Fig. 63.

a. Chest of compressed air. b. Pull-downs of pallets connected with the keys. c. Pallets which admit air into grooves; steadied by moving between two wires. d. Grooves running from back to front under pipes. e. Slider with holes corresponding to pipes, pulled from right to left, so as to admit or prevent admission of air to pipes; connected with the stop-handles.

position by a spring; this is the pallet (c, Fig. 63). Depression of one of the keys pulls down the free end of the pallet and allows air to rush into the pipe. When the finger releases the key, the spring immediately holds the pallet tightly against the orifice.

But to have a pallet under every pipe in a large organ would be an absurdity; therefore, in arranging two sets of pipes, those giving the same note (or likely to be required for simultaneous use) are placed behind one another over the groove into which the pallet admits the air.   If now a key is struck, the pipes which give the same note in both our stops will be sounding at once.   Hence the necessity for our slider-action, which is constructed thus : A strip of wood runs continuously under each row of pipes, having holes at distances exactly corresponding to the distances between the feet of the pipes.   If we push this strip, which is called the *slider*, into such a position that its perforations and the openings leading to the feet of the pipes exactly coincide, then air can pass into the pipes when the pallet opens.   If, on the contrary, we push this strip of wood so that none of its perforations coincide with the entrances to the feet of the pipes, no air can reach a pipe, even if the pallet be opened.   In the former case we say a stop is *out*, in the latter that it is *in*. The diagram (*see* previous page, Fig. 63) will make all this easily understood.

How simple are these two great constructive principles of the organ ! Had they been appreciated by the Ancients, there would seem to have been no obstacle to their building organs of any magnitude ; for the modern organ with its three or four manuals in tiers, and its pedal-organ, is nothing more than a collection of as many organs all built on these two principles ; and, as before remarked, the ability and ingenuity of modern organ-builders have been directed more to the easiest means of bringing these manifold organs under one performer's control than to the discovery of a radical alteration in the principles of their construction.

Who can venture to say that these simple principles were never mastered by the Ancients? If the reader will turn back to our mention of the *magrepha*, he will find that such contrivances must have been known at least as early as the 2nd century; and there seems little reason to believe that any sudden and unexpected discovery led to their adoption. In the case of all other musical instruments, a gradual but very perceptible growth in the ingenuity of their construction is to be traced. Why not so with the *ugab*? The only conclusion to be drawn from all this is that the *ugab* must be considered as an instrument of importance and magnitude in direct proportion to the period of its existence. To some this may seem a very contemptible conclusion, but it is not so. The use of the word extends over a vast period, and those writers, therefore, who consider that it denotes but one unvaried, unchanging instrument are, judging from what the history of music teaches us, treading on untenable ground.

It is remarkable that the latest improvements in the construction of the organ should have been in its bellows. One would have supposed that so important an element in its existence would have been perfected early in its use. Such, however, is not the case. It must be generally known that as the top of a common bellows, such as a blacksmith's, descends if left to itself, the pressure on the air contained inside it increases, because the weight of the top and sides is resting upon a constantly diminishing quantity and therefore surface of air. It is also a well-known fact that organ-pipes change in their pitch to a considerable extent, according to the pressure of the air which is passing through them. The Ancients, then, if they had only one such simply-formed bellows, could have produced no sounds at all while the top of the bellows was being raised by the blower, as this process took off the pressure on the inside air ; and even supposing that several such bellows were adapted to one organ in such a manner that while the contents of some were being utilised by the organist the others were being re-filled, the pressure of the air must nevertheless have been far from constant, unless the ingenuity of the blowers counteracted the influence of natural laws.   A glance at Fig. 60, on page 122, will show this clearly.   These old-fashioned bellows were called diagonal.   The bellows of modern organs, called horizontal, practically consist of the old kind of bellows (now called the feeders) *and* a reservoir just above them, which, owing to valves at its underside, cannot drop while the feeders are being replenished.   And in order still further to equalise the pressure, the ribs of our bellows are so arranged that while one set meet inwardly the others meet outwardly.   It seems almost surprising that horizontal bellows were not made until the 16th century.   Some ascribe their introduction to Lobinger, of Nuremberg, in 1570.

The Saxon name for a bellows was *Bilig* or *Blast-belg ;* similar to it is the old German *Blasebalg.* Hence a bellows-blower was called a bellows-treader (*Balgentreter*).   Fig. 64, in which this process is rather amusingly illustrated, is given by Dr. Rimbault, from Coussemaker's article in Didron's *Annales Archéologiques.* The awkward pause which must have taken place when the weight of the *treaders* had emptied the bellows, and before it was refilled, can be imagined. The diagonal bellows and their treaders remained in existence quite up to the end of the 18th century. The organ in the comparatively modern cathedral of St. Paul's, London, was blown after this fashion. It possessed four such bellows, each measuring 8 ft. by 4 ft. But other large organs had as many as eight, ten, twelve, and even fourteen. The bellows-treader used to walk leisurely along, and throw his weight upon them in rotation. To this

Fig. 64.

day some Continental organs are blown by the weight of the blower's body, although the bellows themselves are of a modern form of construction. It would be quite unfair to the reader to leave the subject of ancient organs without saying a few words on the much - discussed *water - organ* or *hydraulic-organ*, which is carefully described by Vitruvius Pollio, the celebrated architect of the Augustan era. As explanatory drawings were not fashionable in those days, it is quite impossible to discover what his elaborate and lengthy description really portrays.* But there can be no doubt that the lasting popularity of water-organs was owing to the fact that, by some agency of water, the pressure of the air was equalised, and the defects just noticed as incidental to diagonal bellows remedied. Considering the natural dread which a modern organ-builder has to the approach of water to his instrument, although he is content to work a hydraulic-engine and fill his bellows at a distance, the reader may well wonder how and why ancient organ-builders courted the use of this hostile element. Assuming that the builders of water-organs were aware of that property of water which makes it, if enclosed in a small tube passing downwards and into the base of a vessel of any given area, able to exert on every portion of that area equal to itself any weight equal to that added to itself, we can, perhaps, offer some such explanation of their mechanism as the following :—Suppose two oblong reservoirs of air to be made with their tops fixed, but with movable bottoms, and joined together with a cross-bar in such a manner that the bottom of one must rise as the bottom of the other falls ; suppose also that ordinary valves are placed in the top of each, so that as the bottom rises the valves close, and the air can only escape through a passage into the box on which stand the pipes ; while, on the other hand, as the bottom falls the valves also drop, and admit a fresh supply of air through their openings : Now, if enclosed water were to be admitted below the bottoms of

* Though the principle and structure of the water-organ are now well known, and are fully explained in Supplementary Note (2) to this Chapter, Dr. Stainer's suggestions are interesting and have been retained as they appeared in the original edition.

the reservoirs with a mechanical arrangement which should not only stop the supply of compressed water when the bottom of each reservoir had reached its highest point, but also let the water escape through a waste-valve at the same time, it is not difficult to conceive of a very equal and strong supply of air being sent to the pipes as the two reservoirs were filled and emptied in turn. So long as the water continued to be pumped to the higher level, so long would the supply of air last. There is much in the account of the instrument, as given by Vitruvius, which carries out this view, but parts of his description are unquestionably somewhat figurative. In opposition to the explanation of water-organs here attempted, it may be urged that had the Romans been aware of the peculiar properties consequent on the gravity of liquids, they would never have taken the trouble to build, as they did, massive and beautiful aqueducts when a closed pipe or tube would not only have brought the water safely down into the valley, but up the other hill-side to the same level. Also, that a hydraulic-organ is sometimes spoken of as playing by itself, and how can this be made consistent with the account here given, unless the organ-blower used to be considered the real player, while the man at the pipes was looked upon as a mere nonentity? And, again, it is occasionally mentioned that these instruments were worked by hot water, and if the water were simply used to obtain a force from its special laws of gravity, why, we may ask, need it first be boiled?

Another explanation of the structure of a water-organ may be hazarded. If into a perfectly closed chamber of air a water-pipe is introduced, the air will, of course, be compressed in proportion to the quantity of water forced in. If pipes were placed over such a chamber, with a slider under each pipe, under the control of the player, the admission of the air from the chamber would unquestionably

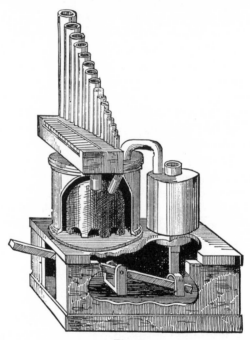

Fig. 65.

cause them to speak, and with two such chambers a tolerably constant supply of compressed air could be obtained, one providing this while the other was being emptied of its water.

This digression on the hydraulic organ is not altogether out of place here, as enthusiasts are not wanting who would make us believe that this instrument was among those known and used by the Jews in their Temple worship.* Several authors have attempted to give pictures of it, and, it is not too much to say, have seriously taxed their inventive powers in so doing. Among them may be quoted Kircher, Isaac Vossius, Perrault (*Commentary on Vitruvius*), and Optantianus. A rude representation of one is also to be seen on a coin of the time of Nero, preserved in the Vatican. That given in Fig. 65 is from Häuser's *Kirchen Musik*, and is to be found, with much more valuable information, including the text of Vitruvius's account, in Rimbault's well-known *History of the Organ.* It is probably purely fanciful; the reader is therefore likely to be, after studying it carefully, no wiser than he was before.†

If we turn to that nation whose careful preservation of old traditions in art renders their present customs unusually valuable—the Chinese —we are struck by a remarkable fact, namely, that the organ they use is constructed on a totally different principle from that which has grown up in Europe. It is blown by being placed against the mouth of the performer, a truly primitive method, and one which, if adhered to, must have utterly prevented any great improvements in the instrument. The player finds room to pass his hand round into the back of the instrument, and so reaches the pipes which he has to stop, for by stopping the holes, and inhaling the wind, the pipes are made to speak.

* Chappell states that it was invented in the third century B.C. See his *History of Music*, p. 326.

† See, however, Supplementary Note (2), to this Chapter.

Fig. 66 represents a *cheng* or Chinese organ, and in Fig. 67 is shown the position in which it is held when in use.   The most important difference between the *cheng* and our organ is that its sounds

Fig. 66.

are produced by *free reeds*.   The method by which sound is produced in an ordinary reed-stop on the organ is this: the metal tongue of the reed is rather larger than the orifice through which the air is forced, and is slightly curved at its extremity. When, therefore, the current of air is directed to it the tongue is forced down over the orifice,

Fig. 67.

but its own elasticity causes it to return, when the air again forces it down, and so on; the number of these backward and forward motions being of course the number of vibrations necessary to produce the particular sound required. But in the case of the free reed, the tongue is not so large as the orifice through which the air is forced; when, therefore, the current of air is directed against it, it bends, and passes through the opening, but is immediately restored to its position, as in the ordinary reed, by its own elasticity. That is to say, the tongue of the common reed beats against the opening, that of the free reed passes in and out of it. It is almost incredible that such a simple source of obtaining sweet sounds should have remained so long unused in Europe. It is said that an organ-builder, by name Kratzenstein, of St. Petersburg, saw a *cheng*, and made some organ stops on this principle, about the middle of the 18th century. But the real value of free reeds does not seem to have been appreciated until Grenié, of Paris, in 1810, discarded the pipes and used the reeds alone, thus inventing the harmonium. Perhaps few of the many thousands who play upon this cheap and now sweet-toned instrument are aware that it is a true descendant of the *cheng*. Accordions and concertinas form the connecting link between the *cheng* and harmonium, as they combine the portability and free reeds of the former with the bellows-system of the latter. The *cheng* contains from thirteen to twenty-one pipes, and is probably one of the oldest wind-instruments now in use. Some have gone so far as to call it "Jubal's organ," but had it been in use among the Jews, it is difficult to believe that all traces of it would be lost among the nations which were in close contact and inter-communication with them, especially as it is exceedingly light and

easily carried, and would therefore in all probability have been preserved by them in their
wanderings and captivities. It is improbable,
therefore, that the *cheng*, ancient as is its origin,
is allied to the Hebrew *ugab*, and the latter was
probably in the earliest times a collection of pipes
of the very simplest character, but growing into
more importance as from time to time improvements were made in its construction. We have
seen that the Jews were not unwilling to adopt the
improved form of stringed instruments which they
sometimes found in neighbouring nations, and there
is no special reason for supposing that in the case
of the *ugab* no attempts were made to improve
upon the form invented by Jubal. An organ, in
our modern sense of the name, it hardly could
have been, unless keys were invented by the
Ancients ; but a collection of pipes it certainly was,
which could be made to sound at the will of the
player, albeit, perhaps, by clumsy mechanism.
In the Septuagint the word *ugab* has three
distinct renderings—κιθάρα (*kithara*) in Gen. iv. 21 ;
ψαλμός (*psalmos*) in Job xxi. 12, and xxx. 31 ; and
ὄργανον (*organon*) in Ps. cl. 4. That Biblical
scholars should have ventured to translate one
Hebrew word by three names of such totally
different significations as " guitar," " psaltery,"
" organ," is a sufficient warning to us of the danger
of trusting to translations. In our Authorised
Version it is uniformly rendered as " organ "—
" Such as handle the harp and organ " (Gen. iv.
21) ; " Rejoice at the sound of the organ " (Job xxi.
12) ; " My harp (*kinnor*) also is turned to mourning,
and my organ (*ugab*) into the voice of them
that weep " (Job xxx. 31) ; " Praise him with

stringed-instruments and organs " (Ps. cl. 4).   But in the Prayer-book Version it is in this last passage rendered by " pipe " : " Praise him upon the strings (*minnim*) and pipe (*ugab*)." Here the word is perhaps used to express wind - instruments generally : " Praise Him with stringed instruments and wind instruments." The German version of the Bible translates *ugab* in every case by " pipes " (*Pfeifen*).

As organs form in our days such an important element in the musical part of Christian worship, a few words on the probable date of their dedication to this sacred function may not be unwelcome.   It is generally said that they were introduced into Church services by Pope Vitalianus in the 7th century.   But on the other hand, mention is found of an organ which belonged to a church of nuns at Grado before the year 580.   This instrument has even been minutely described as having been 2 ft. long by 6 in. deep, and as possessing thirty pipes, acted upon by fifteen keys or slides.   It seems to be tolerably authenticated that one was sent by Constantine in 766 as a present to Pepin, King of France.   Improvements in their construction are attributed to Pope Sylvester, who died 1003.   When we reach the time of Chaucer their use must have been common, for he thus speaks in his *Nonnes Preestes Tale* (Nun Priest's Tale) of a crowing cock " highte chaunticlere " :

> " His vois was merier than the mery orgon
> On masse daies that in the chirches gon."

The very existence of organs was imperilled in the troublous times of the Rebellion, and Puritans were no friends to their re-introduction.

Opinions differ as to the derivation of the word *ugab*.   Buxtorf traces it to a root *agabh*, which signifies " to love," and therefore defines it as " instrumentum musicum, quasi *amabile* dictum." By another author it is derived from an Arabic root *akab*, " to blow." The only passages in Holy Scripture in which the *ugab* is mentioned are those above quoted.

Mashrokitha or *mishrokitha* is the name of a musical instrument mentioned only in verses 5, 7, 10, and 15 of the 3rd chapter of Daniel. It has been described by different writers as a double-flute, Pan's-pipe, and also an organ. As an example of the thoughtless manner in which illustrations are appended to supposed descriptions of ancient musical instruments, it may be mentioned that the figure of a *magrepha*, as given by Gaspar Printz (1690) has been copied in a well-known work on Biblical literature as an illustration of a *mashrokitha*. Considering that these instruments had not only no claim to similarity of construction, but also were used by two distinct nations at an interval of about 600 years, the appropriateness of the figure of one (which by the way was in the first instance purely imaginary) as an illustration of the form of the other, to say the least is somewhat remote. The word *mashrokitha* is traced to a root *sharak*, " to hiss " (*sibilare*), and as a certain amount of hissing necessarily accompanies the use of the Pan's-pipe, the *mashrokitha* has generally been thought to be an instrument of that class. It is indeed rendered in the Greek by σῦριγξ (*syrinx*). The fact that the Hebrew translation of *mashrokitha* was *ugab* does not go to prove that the *ugab* was a *syrinx*, as we have had sufficient doubt thrown on the trustworthiness of translators by the manifold renderings of *ugab* itself.

Supplementary Notes.

(1.) As already observed in the Supplementary Note (2) appended to the preceding chapter, the vertically-blown flute is ethnographically and historically distinct from the side-blown type though the sounding principle is the same. The Pan's-pipe is simply a collection of vertical flutes, blown across the open ends, and when to the single vertical flute an automatic device was adapted for directing the breath of the player on to the edge of the tube (which in time produced the well-known whistle-head) it was only natural that the same improvement would be embodied in a series of pipes, giving us the organ, as the earlier grouping had produced the Pan's-pipe. It is quite likely that the "sweet" Greek *monaulos* was furnished with some kind of whistle-head, though the present Greek *aulos* still remains a simple vertical flute. At the commencement of our era the Græco-Roman world was certainly quite familiar with the whistle-head as we see it in the organ-pipe.

(2.) The principle and construction of the *hydraulus* or water-organ are now perfectly understood, principally owing to discoveries made on the site of ancient Carthage, where small models in baked clay have been found, which, with the help of the explanatory treatises of Hero (3rd century B.C.), Vitruvius (*c.* 15 B.C.) and recently of M. Loret, have enabled the present writer to construct a working facsimile of the instrument. The find of most importance in this connection was that of a pottery representation of the *hydraulus* and a performer on it, almost perfect and a little over seven inches in height. Hitherto mosaics and coins had shown only the front view of the instrument, but in this specimen the whole was of course displayed (Plate VII.).

The mechanism can best be explained by reference to the accompanying diagrams (Figs. 68A and 68B), drawn from the working reproduction (Plates VIII., IX.). On either

VII. THE WATER ORGAN (HYDRAULUS).—GRÆCO-ROMAN ART: *c.* 120 A.D. (p. 140.)

VIII. THE WATER ORGAN (HYDRAULUS).—WORKING REPRODUCTION.
FRONT VIEW. (p. 140.)

IX. THE WATER ORGAN (HYDRAULUS).—WORKING REPRODUCTION.
BACK VIEW. (p. 140.)

side of the organ are two barrel-shaped air pumps (A) fitted
with a plunger (B) and an intake valve (C).   These pumps,
raised alternately by levers, each with a long handle centred
at (D), force air through the pipe (E) and the valve (F) into

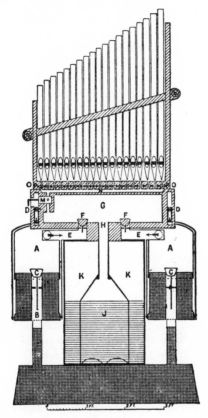

Fig. 68A.

the wooden wind-chest (G): finding no outlet owing to
the closing of the valves, the air passes down the tube (H)
into a metal retainer (J), funnel-shaped and raised on
short feet. This retainer stands in water which is contained

in the cistern (K), and as the air enters from the wind-chest the water is forced out and rises in the cistern: thus, owing to the displacement of the water, the air both in the retainer and in the wind-chest above is subject to heavy pressure.

On the upper side of the top board of the wind-chest three channels (N) are cut, each communicating at one end with the interior of the chest by means of a hole, closed by a cylindrical tap-shaped stop (M), which when turned admits the air to the channel above. Covering the whole length of these air-channels is a double board (O)—divided into lower and upper boards,—between which slide small slips of metal (P) pierced with holes to correspond to the air-holes in the boards, each being furnished with a stop-block (Q)—see Fig. 68B. In their normal position, however, the metal sliders are drawn out so that their solid surface covers the holes and bars the egress of the air: but, when pushed in to the pin (R), their holes correspond to those in the lower and upper boards, and the air under the pressure of the water rushes through into the pipes which stand immediately above the sliders, and the organ speaks. It would be possible to work the pushing-in and drawing-out of the sliders by the two hands, as was done in the pneumatic organs of mediæval times (Figs. 59, 60), but the Greeks and Romans were more advanced than that: they made use of a hinged or centred key (s t u), which when pressed down by the finger, pushed in the slider (P), its return to the closed position being ensured by a spring (V), in earlier times of horn and in later days of metal. The compass of the keyboard of the Carthage *Hydraulus* (*c.* 120 A.D.) was 19 notes, which, according to the scales used by the water-organists, comprised the following (beginning from Bass G): G, A, B flat, B natural, C, D, E flat, E natural, F, F sharp, G, G sharp, A, B flat, B natural, C, C sharp, D, and E. The three ranks of pipes were of unison, octave and super-octave pitch: by means of the stops mentioned above they could be added or silenced at will, another refinement unknown to the mediæval organs; they could also be tuned by means of sliding stoppers (W), or by open tubes (X) working on

the outside of the pipe.   As I can testify from my own
experience,   quite rapid   music   can   be   performed   on   the

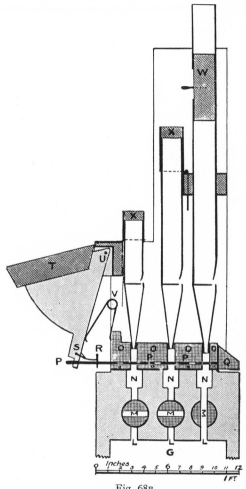

Fig. 68B.

hydraulus,   and   Claudian's   "light touch"   and   "flying
finger" were no mere poetical fancy of the 4th century.

The air-pumps, it is true, require constant working, but the air pressure is well maintained and equalised by the weight of the water.   It is certainly remarkable that the air reservoir now used in our large organs—where the same result produced by the water is obtained by heavy weights of metal—was introduced barely 150 years ago, though something of the kind was to be found in the small chamber organs a century earlier.   It seems very probable that the advanced principles and useful mechanism of the *hydraulus* were lost sight of in the Middle Ages because, being connected with gladiatorial shows and theatrical displays, its use in Christian Churches was not appreciated.   The illustration given in Fig. 61 (p. 122), from the *Eadwine Psalter* of the 12th century, is evidently that of a *water* organ, but it has been copied by the Saxon artist from the *Utrecht Psalter* of 7th century foreign workmanship.

CHAPTER VII.

WIND INSTRUMENTS *(continued).*—SUMPONYAH,
SAMPUNIA, SUMPHONIA, SYMPHONIA.

THIS instrument is among those enumerated in
Dan. iii. 15. In speaking of the *psanterin* or
dulcimer, we had occasion to regret that the word
symphonia should have been translated by
"dulcimer" in our Authorised Version, when
this word would have represented more properly
psanterin. The *symphonia* is now generally
supposed to have been a bagpipe. The reasons
for this belief are, that the meaning of the word,
"sounding together," is not inapplicable to the
union of melody and drone which the latter
instrument produces, and also that the Italians
still have a bagpipe called *sampugna* or *sampogna.*
Of the popularity of the bagpipe there is ample
evidence. Varieties of it seem to have been
common in all parts of Asia and Europe. The
Greeks called it ἀσκαυλος *(ascaulos)*, which means
the "leathern-bottle pipe" (from ἀσκός, a leathern
bag or bottle, and αὐλός, a pipe). The Romans
gave it a name having much the same meaning
—*tibiæ utriculares* or *utricularium;* in Germany it
is the *Sackpfeife,* corresponding exactly to our

bagpipe ; in Italy *sampogna, piva* (in Dan. iii. 5, &c., the Italian translation has *sampogna)*, or *cornamusa,* which last means apparently a hornpipe, alluding probably to the material of which the "pipe" part was sometimes made, not only in Europe, but amongst the Arabians.   From the Italian *cornamusa* the French adopted *cornemuse,* and in both countries the diminutive *musetta* or *musette* (a little *musa* or pipe) seems to have been generally used.   A piece of music written in the style of bagpipe music came afterwards

Fig. 69.

to be called a Musette.   By some it is said also to have been called *chalumeau* by the French ; but it is probable that this name was only so far used in connection with the bagpipe as to describe the pipe or "chanter" pierced with finger-holes, in opposition to that in which the drone-reed was inserted.   The Gaelic name for bagpipe is *biob morh;* the Welsh, *pibau.*   Fig. 69 shows an Arabian instrument of this class, called by them *souqqarah* or *zouggarah.*   It is of goat-skin, and the two pipes with finger-holes are tipped with horn.

The scale consists of four notes, A to D of the treble stave, both pipes being in unison. It will be noticed that the goat-skin reservoir is filled by means of a little tube (seen on the left-hand side of the illustration), which is placed in the mouth of the performer. There are, in fact, two kinds of bagpipe, if viewed as to their construction. In the one the reservoir is supplied from the mouth of the performer, who blows into it through the tube or

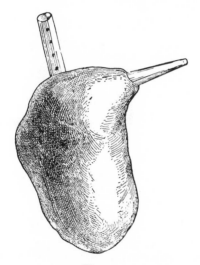

Fig. 70.

mouthpiece; in the other bellows are provided so that the pressure of the right elbow against the side will force the air which they contain into the reservoir placed under the left arm. It will be seen that the *souqqarah* (Fig. 69) belongs to the former of these kinds. The bagpipe shown in Fig. 70, which is an Indian instrument called *tourti* or *tourry*, is of the same kind, the inflation of the reservoir being brought about through the mouthpiece. That its chanter has only four holes is probably a proof of its great antiquity. Another instrument of the same sort, called a *zitty*, has seven holes. So, too, the *magoudi* (Fig. 71), used by the Indian snake-charmers when they

Fig, 71.

exhibit their almost Orphean influence over the reptiles, is supplied with air from the mouth, only in this case there is no compressible bag. The reservoir is made of the outer coating of a gourd, the small end of which is pierced for the admission of the air. The two pipes appear each to have four holes, but one has seven, three more being pierced on the reverse side. The tone is said to be soft and somewhat sweet.

The Persians have their *nay* or *neï-ambanah*, which, though to some extent different in form, is of the same construction as a bagpipe.

It is interesting to note the close relationship between the *arghool* of the Egyptians, as before described (pp. 105, 106), and the *souqqarah*. The reservoir is the only distinctive feature of the *souqqarah*, for the *arghool* is of two kinds, like its relations of the bagpipe family; having in some cases two pipes tuned to two unison scales, in others, two pipes, one for the playing of a tune, the other for a drone or bourdon.

The broad distinction between bagpipes blown by means of the mouth and those blown by "pumping" with the elbow, before mentioned, is, however, exhibited much nearer home. Irish bagpipes are inflated by elbow-bellows, Scotch by the mouth. Both have their special advocates, but it is said that the most ancient Irish instruments of this class were blown, like the Scotch, by the mouth. The Irish lay claim to the superiority of their bagpipes on the ground of the tenor chords which they are capable of producing.

The *sampogna*, the modern Italian form of the Roman *utricularium*, is commonly played on the Campagna and the surrounding hills. Fétis remarks that when some of these poor *sampognatori* or *sampognari* migrated to Paris some years ago, in the hopes of getting a livelihood, they were popularly called *pifferari*, but, of course, wrongly so, as the *pifferari* are oboists, not bagpipers.

Some are occasionally to be seen about the streets of London.

The early traces of this instrument are unfortunately very scanty. An example, found in Silicia, is said to be shown in Fig. 72, but the reader will probably think that it might with equal justice be said to represent many other things.* The Phœnicians were well acquainted with bagpipes; hence it is probable that this is the source from whence the Greeks obtained them, or imitated their method of construction, and that the Romans

Fig. 72.

copied them from the Greeks. The Syrian Greeks called it σαμπονία (samponia), and the question at once arises, Was this an imitation of sumponyah, a genuine Chaldaic name, or were both samponia and soumponiah corruptions of the Greek symphonia (συμφωνία); or, to put the question in other words, did the Greeks give Greek names to Chaldee musical instruments, or did the Chaldees borrow their instruments from Greece? This difficulty has been alluded to on page 52 in Chap. iii. It is completely out of the sphere of the musician, and

* See Supplementary Note (2), to this Chapter.

must be left for scholars and theologians to settle, or perhaps it would be safer to say, to discuss.   As the *symphonia* is only mentioned in that catalogue of musical instruments given in Dan. iii. with such strange iteration, it must be presumed that the captive Jews did not so highly value its merits as to wish to adopt it.   But harsh as the tones of a bagpipe are when heard in a small enclosed place, there can be no two opinions as to the romantic and beautiful effect they produce when heard in the midst of wild scenery; and when large numbers are played together the result is even imposing and grand.   The repetition of the phrase " all kinds of musick" (Dan. iii. 5, 7, 10, 15) would lead us to believe that a very large company of musicians was gathered together on that memorable day when Nebuchadnezzar tried to enforce idol-worship; but though the instruments themselves were of a barbarous type, we may still believe that the massive volume of sound produced by so many playing together must have been awe-inspiring and terrific.

Supplementary Notes.

(1.)   The division of bagpipes into those played directly from the mouth and those played by bellows beneath the arm is arbitrary and likely to cause confusion, because in many cases the attachment of the bellows is merely temporary and for a passing convenience.   It is more interesting and important to observe the forms of reed used in the chanters or melody pipes.   In the Arabian *souqqarah*, for instance, and in the pipes of the Greek Islands, the reeds are of the single-beating or clarinet type, being derived from the *arghool* (Fig. 52); whereas in the Indian pipes and in the European forms the reeds are of the double or oboe type.   In the Indian *magoudi* or *poongi*, however, shown in Fig. 71, which has no bag, but a gourd reservoir for the air, the single-beating reed is employed, and in the old Keltic *pibgorn* or hornpipe the same type of reed is found. Similar reeds are also used for the drones of the Irish and Scotch pipes.

(2.) During a series of excavations in Persia some terra-cotta figures were discovered in a mound at Susa, and two of them appear to be performing on bagpipes, the chanter being curved. They are supposed to be of the 8th century B.C., and are illustrated in M. J. de Morgan's *Délégation en Perse* (1900). According to Prof. Garstang (*The Land of the Hittites*), one of the figures on the sculptured slab found in the old Hittite palace at Eyuk (Plate III.) is playing on a bagpipe; but it seems very questionable, and more probably represents a jester with a performing monkey. A somewhat similar scene of court performers, with an accompanying guitar-player, was sculptured on the walls of the ancient palace of Nimroud.

Early bagpipes were always made without the drone-pipe: the single drone appears in Europe about the 13th century and two drone pipes a century later.

CHAPTER VIII.

WIND INSTRUMENTS (*continued*).—KEREN, SHOPHAR, KHATSOTSRAH.

THESE are the names of the three important Hebrew trumpets. The first, at any rate in its primitive form, was constructed from the natural horn of an animal. *Keren* and *shophar* are sometimes used synonymously, notably so in the account of the capture of Jericho (Josh. vi.) But in this same account there is affixed to *keren* the word *jobel*, making the whole a "jobel-horn." Although this is translated "ram's horn" in our version, and although it has been suggested that *jobel* in Arabic, if not in Hebrew, might signify a ram, yet on the whole it seems probable that *jobel* is the source of our word *jubilee*, and that the expression simply points to the fact that the instrument was used on great solemnities, and was a *jubilee-trumpet*. The actual horns of animals were in very early times imitated in metal or ivory. In the latter case a tusk was hollowed out and often elaborately carved. They were called in the Middle Ages *oliphants*, or elephant-trumpets, from their material. The Ashantees to this day use tusks for this purpose, only, strangely enough, the instrument is blown through a hole in the side and not at the small end. In 1 Chron. xxv., after giving a list of those set aside by David to play upon the *keren*, the historian says, at v. 5, " All these were the sons of Heman, the king's seer in the words of God, to lift up the horn." Again, translated in our version by " cornet " (though in the Septuagint by σάλπιγξ), the word occurs in Dan. iii. 5, &c. Only in these passages (and Lev. xxiii. 24) is the *keren* named as

Fig. 73.

a musical instrument, although the word often occurs with other meanings, and is frequently used as figurative of " strength." In Fig. 73 are shown forms of the *keren;* the straight trumpet is the *khatsotsrah* (p. 157).

The *shophar*, judging from its very frequent mention, extending in the pages of the Bible from the Book of Exodus to that of Zechariah, must have been more commonly used than the *keren*. It was the voice of a *shophar*, exceeding loud, issuing from the thick cloud on Sinai, when, too, thunders and lightnings rolled around the holy mount, which made all in the camp tremble. When Ehud's personal daring had rid Israel of a tyrant, he blew a *shophar* and gathered the people together to seize the fords of Jordan towards Moab. Gideon used the instrument, and Saul also (1 Sam. xiii. 3), and many other of Israel's warriors, to rouse and call up the people against

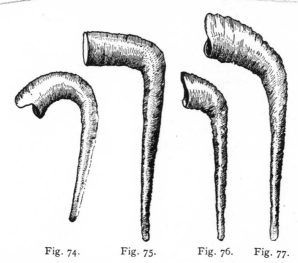

Fig. 74.   Fig. 75.   Fig. 76.   Fig. 77.

their enemies. But it was not confined to military use, for " David and all the house of Israel brought up the Ark of the Lord with shouting, and with the sound of the *shophar*" (2 Sam. vi. 15). It is mentioned three times in the Psalms : " God is gone up with a shout, the Lord with the sound of a trumpet (*shophar*)" (Ps. xlvii. 5); " Blow up the *shophar* in the new moon " (Ps. lxxxi. 3) ; " Praise him with the sound of the *shophar*" (Ps. cl. 3).

The *shophar* is especially interesting to us as being the only Hebrew instrument whose use on certain solemn occasions seems to be retained to this day. Engel, with his usual trustworthy research, has traced out and examined some of these in modern synagogues. That shown in Fig. 74 (p. 155) is from the synagogue of Spanish and Portuguese Jews, Bevis Marks, and is, he says, one foot in length. Fig. 75 shows one used in the Great Synagogue, St. James's Place, Aldgate, twenty-one inches in length. Both are made of horn. Figs. 76 and 77 Engel gives in his valuable *Music of the most Ancient Nations*, from Saalchütz. The first is a ram's horn, the second that of a cow. On these instruments signals or flourishes are on certain occasions played, the music of which it is unnecessary to give, as they are well known as the simplest progressions which such tubes are capable of producing. All such tube-instruments can only give a series of sounds called natural harmonics or over-tones, which are produced by forcing (gradually increasing the pressure of air from the lips) the column of air they contain—in the first instance—into two vibrating parts; then three, four, five, six, and so on.

Here is the series of notes which can be produced by a trumpet of which the fundamental note is C :—

The notes marked * are not in tune with the sounds thus ordinarily represented, and are not therefore used, except among barbarous nations, although sometimes they can be heard in a *Ranz des vaches* or *Kuhreihen* among the Alps.

The relation of the intervals of this series remains unaltered for all open tubes, only the pitch can vary; thus a trumpet in D would give D, D, A, D, F♯, &c. The orchestral trumpeters of the 17th and 18th centuries were able by careful "lipping" to correct the false intonation of the 11th harmonic.

The series of sounds given above (varying in pitch, not in relation) was therefore the actual scale of the *keren*, *shophar*, and *khatsotsrah*.

When a tube-instrument is required on which a chromatic series of sounds can be played, pistons must be used as in our modern cornets, or slides as in our trombones. Tubes with slides are more ancient than is often supposed. Fig. 78 shows Chinese instruments of this class.*

The *khatsotsrah* is generally thought to have been a straight trumpet with a bell, or "pavillon," as it is termed. Moses received specific directions as to making them: "Make thee two trumpets of silver; of a whole piece shalt thou make them: that thou mayest use them for the calling of the assembly, and for the journeying of the camps" (Num. x. 2). In Ps. xcviii. 6 the *khatsotsrah* and *shophar* are brought into juxtaposition: "With *khatsotsrah* and sound of *shophar* make a joyful noise before the Lord the King"; or, as it incorrectly stands in the Prayer-book version, "With trumpets also and shawms," &c.† In

---

* See, however, Supplementary Note (1), to this Chapter.

† The word *shawm* is a corruption of *chalumeau*, and signified a primitive clarinet or oboe. For a fuller account of the *Shophar* see Appendix V.

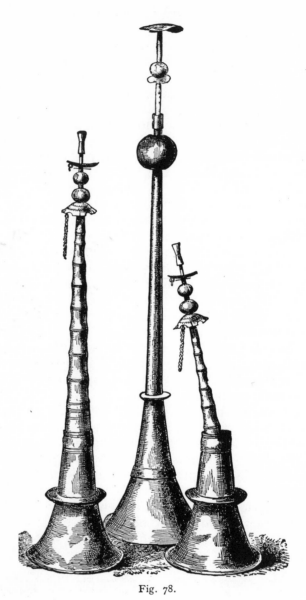

Fig. 78.

this passage the Septuagint has it, 'Εν σάλπιγξιν ἐλαταῖς, κὰι φωνῇ σάλπιγγος κερατίνης, " With ductile trumpets, and the sound of horn-trumpets." So too, the Vulgate: " In tubis ductilibus et voce tubæ corneæ." The word *mikshah*, which is applied to the description of the *khatsotsrah* in Num. x. 2, and means "rounded" or "turned," may apply either to a complete twist in the tube of the instrument, or, what is more probable, to the rounded outline of the bell. But if the former be the real interpretation of the epithet, it would make it more like the large circular horns found at Pompeii—the Roman *bucina*, and similar in form to that depicted on the column of Trajan and many classical monuments. Yet on the other hand the account given by Josephus points out the latter as characteristic of its shape. He says, " Moses invented a kind of trumpet of silver ; in length it was less than a cubit, and it was somewhat thicker than a pipe ; its opening was enlarged, to admit blowing on it with the mouth ; at the lower end it had the form of a bell, like a horn." It seems chiefly to have been brought into use in the Hebrew ritual, but was also frequently a battle-call, and blown on other warlike occasions. It was the sound of the *khatsotsrah* which made the guilty Athaliah tremble for her safety and rend her clothes, crying, " Treason ! treason !" Silver trumpets have always been associated with dignity and grandeur, whether blown before a Pope in the ritual of the great church of St. Peter at Rome, or carried, as in this country, by royal trumpeters, and by a few favoured regimental bands. In Figs. 79 and 80 two coins are shown, on which, surrounded by a motto, "the deliverance of Jerusalem," trumpets are delineated. These instruments have been described as specimens of the *khatsotsrah*, with much probability of truth.

The shape which these sacred trumpets took, at any rate in the Herodian Temple, is well shown on the arch of Titus, where they are placed with the Table of Shewbread and Golden Candlestick amongst the victor's spoils. (See Plate X.)

The Assyrians appear to have used trumpets, as Fig. 81 plainly shows; but there are at present no records of their having trumpets with a distinct bell. Figs. 82 and 83 (p. 162) prove, however, that such terminations to tubes were not unknown to the

Fig. 79.   Fig. 80.

Egyptians. The Romans had at least three varieties of trumpet, the most powerful of which was called *tuba*. It was used as a war-trumpet. Fig. 84, from a bas-relief in the Capitol, exhibits a Roman blowing a trumpet at the triumph of Marcus Aurelius. Ancient trumpets, which were usually formed of one piece only, could not possibly be adjusted to any variety of pitch, and therefore must with difficulty have been associated with other instruments. This difficulty is overcome in modern tube-instruments not having slides or pistons (as, for instance, the simple French horn or

X. The Sacred Trumpets (Arch of Titus, Rome) : *c.* 80 A.D. (p. 160.)

trumpet) by changing the *crook* and so lengthening the tube, or shortening it, as to adjust it to a required pitch.*

The verse of the Psalm before quoted (xcviii. 6) is the only one in which mention of the *khatsotsrah*

Fig. 81.

is made by the Psalmist. The first allusion to this instrument in Holy Scripture is where Moses is commanded to make two of silver (Num. x. 2);

* See Supplementary Note (2), to this Chapter.

the last in Hos. v. 8, where it is used in connection
with the *shophar*, and, with it, is to be blown

Fig. 82.   Fig. 83.

Fig. 84.

as a warning to wicked Israel of the approaching
visitation of God.

SUPPLEMENTARY NOTES.

(1.) It is quite true that the Chinese oboes and trumpets shown in Fig. 78 are made in collapsible sections which will slip into one another, but I am assured by the Rev. A. C. Moule (who from long residence in China and intimate knowledge of the language and people is well qualified to state the fact) that " the sliding tubes of these instruments are not meant to change their notes, but to reduce their length when they are not in use. (*Cf.* his work on " Chinese Musical Instruments " in the *Journal of the North China Branch of the Royal Asiatic Society*, vol. xxxix.) The tube, too, of the long trumpet (*lapa*), for instance, is conical, and unless the inner tube is drawn out to its fullest extent the joint is not air-tight. The sliding tubes of the trombone, on the other hand, are cylindrical, and therefore they retain the air throughout their entire length.

The sackbut or trombone appears to have been evolved during the 13th and 14th centuries in Italy or Southern France. The first step was the folding into three parallel lengths of the long straight tube of the *buzine* (a form of trumpet introduced into Europe from the East during the Crusades). This has given us the now well-known trumpet shape. The second step was the application of a slide to this folded and more portable instrument; at first the slide seems to have been made on one section only of the tube; but very soon two sections were included, and the trombone or great trumpet, strengthened with stays, had by the 16th century assumed its present-day form. The name " sackbut " came into use in England when the instrument was introduced late in the 15th century—probably from Spain,—for in that country "sacabuche" is the name of a kind of pump, and no doubt the action of the trombone-player when shortening and lengthening his slide suggested the nickname. In Germany the old name *Buzaun* (now *Posaune*) was retained, and in Italy it was at one time known as the *tromba spezzata* or " broken trumpet."(*See* Plate XI., 4.)

The phrase *tuba ductilis* ("drawn trumpet"), which occurs in some passages of the Vulgate or Latin version of the Scriptures made in the 4th century, has been thought by some to refer to the trombone; but on reference to the original it will be seen that *ductilis* means the drawing-out of the metal by hammering (our English " beaten work") instead of casting it. We are told, for instance, that the Cherubim were made *ex auro ductili* ("beaten gold"), and there is no reason to suppose that they were collapsible. There is hardly any need to point out that the so-called "sackbut of the 9th century," figured by Engel and others from a MS. in the Public Library at Boulogne-sur-Mer, is in reality an attempt, frequently made at that time, to represent the *sambuca* or small harp already described in Chapter iii. The marvellous Pompeian "trombones," one of which was said to have been presented to King George III., are evidently only the large circular trumpets now gracing the walls of the National Museum at Naples.

(2.) Another very popular method of obtaining the chromatic scale from the simple tube was formerly found in piercing holes in it like those of the flute. This produced the old English cornett, the instrument chosen by the translators of the Bible to represent the word *keren* in Daniel iii. It was made of wood and covered with leather, six holes being provided for the fingers and one at the back for the thumb; sometimes the instruments were curved in shape (It., *Cornetto curvo*), sometimes straight (*Cornetto diritto*); and when the mouthpiece was in one piece with the tube it was known as the mute cornett, from its soft tone. In any case the mouthpiece was very small, but similar in principle to that of the modern cornet. Dr. Stainer's description is appended here because it was placed by him under the heading of pipes, through a mistaken idea, once common, that the instrument was played with a double reed :—

" The *cornetto curvo* seems to have been used in all European countries under different names. Two very

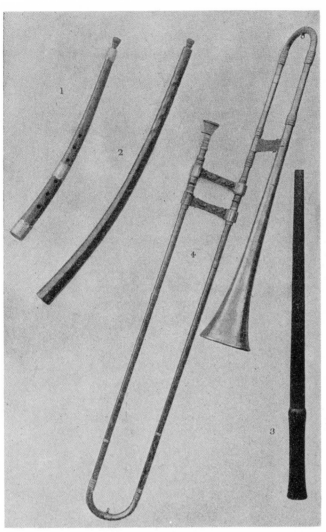

XI. CORNETTS AND SACKBUT.—(GALPIN COLLECTION):
16-17TH CENT. (p. 165.)

beautiful instruments of this kind and shape were discovered in the Cathedral of Christ Church, Oxford, when the muniment-room was being cleared for the purposes of restoration. They were probably in use in the 16th or beginning of the 17th century. Like most *cornetti curvi*, they are made of wood, covered with black leather, but so admirable is the workmanship that a casual glance would lead any one to believe them to be of black wood. They have the usual number of holes, six above and one below, and are elegantly mounted in silver, on which are engraved the arms of the College. They doubtless were the chief support of the treble part, at funerals or any ceremonies where it was necessary to have a musical procession. In Germany (says Engel) they were still employed in the beginning of the 18th century (under the name *Zinken*), when the town bands played chorales, on certain occasions, from the tower of their parish church."

The true bass of the cornett was the serpent, which figured so largely in the regimental bands and the church orchestras of the 18th and early 19th centuries. There is no proof that this side-hole principle was in use on the horns and trumpets of the Hebrews.

On Plate XI. are represented three cornetts and a sackbut in my own collection. No. 1 is the *cornettino curvo* or high treble cornett: it is dated 1518. No. 2 the *cornetto curvo* or treble cornett. No. 3 the *cornetto muto* or mute cornett. No. 4 is a sackbut, the work of Jorg Neuschel of Nuremberg, maker to King Henry VIII. of England: it is dated 1557.

PART III.
INSTRUMENTS OF PERCUSSION.

CHAPTER IX.

TSELTSLIM, OR TZELTZELIM ; METZILLOTH,
OR MTSILTAYIM ; PHA-AMON OR PHAGHAMON.

THE first four words, found about a dozen times
in the Old Testament, are with only one exception
rendered "cymbals" in our version. This name
fully describes the form of the instrument, for
cymbal comes direct from the Greek κύμβαλον
(*cymbalum*), which in turn comes from κύμβος
(*cymbus*), a hollowed plate or basin.

Now, although there are in use among most
nations a large number of varieties of this
instrument, differing in *size*, yet there are only two
having any broad distinction in *form*. Of these,
the one is almost identical with our modern
soup-plate (having a somewhat larger rim) ; the
other has a hollow commencing at the very rim,
and terminating in an upright handle, giving it the
appearance of a hollow cone surmounted by a
handle. Both sorts were in use among the Assyrians.
The comparatively flat cymbals are played by

bringing the right and left hands, each of which held one plate, sharply together at right angles with the body. Of the conical-shaped cymbals, one is held stationary in the left hand, while the other is dashed upon it vertically with the right hand. Fig. 85 shows an Assyrian in the act of striking this last-mentioned form of the instrument. Sculpture also shows people striking the flatter instruments in the manner above described. The

Fig. 85.

ancient Egyptians also used cymbals made of copper with a small admixture of silver. Most fortunately a pair of these was discovered in the tomb of a priestly musician named Ankhapê, close by his mummied body. These are given in Fig. 86. The perforation in the top is, of course, for the purpose of passing through a loop of cord to serve as a handle. A leather strap is used for this purpose in modern instruments. These ancient specimens are about five inches in diameter, and are said to be almost identical, both in form and size, with those used in Egypt at the present time.

In Ps. cl. 5 two sorts are evidently pointed out : " Praise him upon the loud cymbals ; praise him upon the high-sounding cymbals." Bearing this in mind, it is very interesting to find that the Arabs have two distinct varieties, large and small ; for the

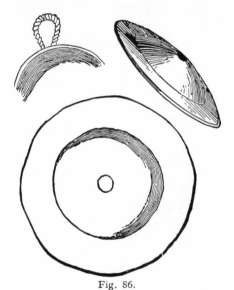

Fig. 86.

" loud cymbals " of the Psalmist would certainly be of a larger diameter than the " high-sounding " cymbals. In the Prayer-book version of this Psalm, the real distinction between these two species is unfortunately not made plain : " Praise him upon the well-tuned cymbals ; praise him upon the loud cymbals." The Arabs use their large cymbals in religious ceremonies, but the

smaller kind seem to be almost limited to the
accompaniment of dances. In India, instruments
of this class are called *talan.* There is also a
smaller species called *kintal.* The Bayadères
dance to the *tal.*

The Turks, as would be expected from their
early origin amongst the tablelands of central
Asia, inherit a system of music chiefly founded on

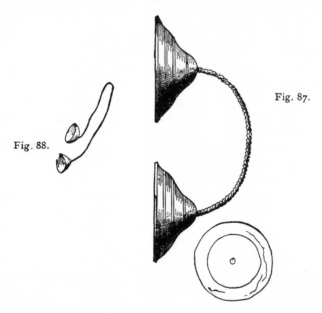

Fig. 87.

Fig. 88.

that of the ancient Persians. They have always
excelled, not only in the use of instruments of
percussion, but also in their construction. From
the fact that the foot-guards of the Sultan were
formerly called Janissaries, music chiefly consisting
of a combination of the sounds of instruments of
percussion has been called " janissary music."

The efforts of Frederick II. to obtain genuine music of this sort for German use are well known. Turkish cymbals still hold a high value, and are manufactured in that country in very large quantities, for exportation westward.

Gongs, though perhaps less strictly musical instruments than cymbals, must be classified with them; and many nations celebrated for the manufacture of one, are equally famous for producing the other. The Chinese and Burmese, for instance, use both cymbals and gongs, their gongs being sometimes suspended on cords in a series of different sizes, so as to produce their national scale when struck in succession.

Fig. 87 shows a specimen of Indian cymbals; Fig. 88, one from Burmah. The joining together of the two plates by means of a cord does not appear to have been at any time a common custom in Europe.

The Greeks and Romans, by whom cymbals seem to have been shaped strictly in accordance with what the name implies—hollow hemispheres of metal,—used them in the rites connected with the worship of Bacchus, Juno, and Cybele. But, as has happened in other cases, the name *cymbal* has been in the most extraordinary way applied to instruments of a totally different construction. The Italians, at one period, called a common tambourine by this name, and even went so far as to apply it to the dulcimer! We have in a previous chapter traced the growth of a dulcimer through various stages, till it reached the form of a harpsichord; the reader, therefore, will not be astonished to find, at a later date, "cymbal" used for harpsichord. But this is not all. As the pianoforte was the direct offspring of the harpsichord, the pianoforte part in a full score is to this day sometimes marked *cembalo*, or " the cymbal part." It seems to be a matter for much regret that musicians should feel bound, by habit or fashion, thus to perpetuate a title which is not only unmeaning, but absolutely incorrect. It is difficult to understand in what respect the dulcimer was thought to bear any resemblance to cymbals. Some say that because it was struck with hammers it might with justice be called an instrument of percussion ; but it is more probable that the peculiar clang caused by hitting wire strings with little wooden mallets, gave some fanciful resemblance between the " ringing " tone of both instruments.* In modern military bands, cymbals are used as of old, a plate being held firmly in each hand by a leather thong, and by swinging the hands together the plates clash. In modern orchestras the instrument is generally used thus : one plate is horizontally fixed (rather loosely) on to the top of an upright drum ; with his left hand the player holds the other plate, and with his right hand a drumstick. Thus, not only can one performer play both instruments simultaneously, but the tone and clang of the cymbals are much intensified by being in close connection with the vibrating skin and frame of the drum.

Cymbals, in a somewhat unexpected manner, came to be associated with the tambour. For as they became reduced in size it was found possible to insert several pairs inside the rim of the tambour, so that their clatter should either join in the rhythmical beating of the tambour, or be

* See Supplementary Note (2), to this Chapter.

heard alone when the tambour is held by one hand, and shaken rapidly. These *petites cymbales* were occasionally fixed to the thumb and forefinger of both hands, which were then clapped together, as shown in Fig. 89. Hence they came to be called *castanets*, from their similarity to the old toy—hardly worthy of the name of a musical instrument, although it was used with dancing—which consisted of *chestnuts* attached to the fingers (as in Fig. 89), and beaten together, the words *chestnuts* and *castanets* both being derived from *castanea* (Lat.) and κάστανον (Greek), the name of the tree. But in process of time, pieces of ivory or

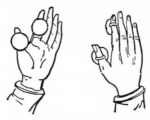

Fig. 89.

mother-of-pearl were substituted for chestnuts. Hence the bones which we see rattled between the fingers of quasi-negro minstrels are dignified with the name castanets, and can in some sense trace their pedigree to the ancient cymbals. Hence, too, we get an explanation of the old word *nakers* or *nackers*, which was applied to castanets by Chaucer, and used commonly at a later period. Evidently it alludes to the material of which they were made, *nacre* being the French, and *nacar* the Spanish for "mother-of-pearl." * Very small cymbals have

* See, however, Supplementary Note (2), to this Chapter.

occasionally been used in the modern orchestra. Berlioz, who gave so much attention, and devoted so much talent, to the increasing of the resources of a band, used, in a symphony, a pair not bigger than the palm of the hand, and tuned them at an interval of a fifth apart. It should be stated that in playing cymbals, not only in Europe, but in Asia, it is not usual to strike them edge against edge, as the Assyrian appears to be doing with his conical cymbals in Fig. 85, but to make one plate only partially overlap the other. If the former method be adopted, the vibrations of the plates are very liable to destroy each other, owing to the extent of the contact of the two surfaces; if the latter, the plates have more "play" when in vibration.

In the Holy Scriptures the use of cymbals is solely confined to religious ceremonies—the bringing back of the Ark from Kirjath-jearim (1 Chron. xv. 16, 19, 28); at the dedication of Solomon's Temple (2 Chron. v. 13); at the restoration of worship by Hezekiah (2 Chron. xxix. 25); at the laying of the foundation of the second Temple (Ezra iii. 10); and at the dedication of the wall of Jerusalem (Neh. xii. 27). This would lead us to suppose that cymbals were not commonly used among the Jews as an accompaniment to dancing. Certain Levites were set aside as cymbalists, as described in 1 Chron. xvi. 42, and elsewhere. They are mentioned in Ezra iii. 10, as being used with trumpets (*khatsotsrah*) only, but in most other instances are described as being used with harps and other Hebrew instruments. There is deep meaning in the allusion of St. Paul to the cymbals in 1 Cor. xiii. 1. Inasmuch as they give out a shrill and clanging sound (κύμβαλον ἀλαλάζον), and are incapable of being tempered or tuned so as to form ever-varied chords with those musical instruments which surround them, they too well illustrate the hollowness and emptiness of character which, while making noble professions with the tongue, lacks that gift of charity which, if it truly glowed in us all, would soon attune all the discords of this world into such a sweet harmony as were worthy of heaven itself. It is a pity that ἀλαλάζον should in that fine passage have been translated "tinkling," a word now used to describe any trifling, petty jingle; it should have been "a clanging" or "clashing cymbal."

The only instance in which one of these related words (viz., *metzilloth*) is translated otherwise than by "cymbals," occurs in Zech. xiv. 20, where it is rendered by "bells": "In that day shall there be upon the bells of the horses, HOLINESS UNTO THE LORD." The margin here has another reading—"upon the *bridles* of the horses." But if the word be understood in a musical sense or not, it can in no way be considered as badly rendered by "bells," for the Eastern custom of having little plates of metal attached to the caparisons of horses so as to produce a jingling noise is well known. And if these plates had circular indentations they would be little cymbals; and if these indentations be made deeper and wider until the flat part disappears, little bells are the result. This gradual change of metal plates into bells is interesting and important. The indentation of cymbals would be found to add to their vibrating power and sonority, and as this indentation became

exaggerated, nothing would be more probable than
that they should eventually be formed into half-
globes. This form, as before has been remarked,
is actually to be found in Roman and Greek
sculpture. Then again, in course of time, these
half-globes or, as they might truly be called, these
hemispherical *bells*, would be found to be shrill and
noisy in tone. Hence there would naturally follow
the experiments, as made in Europe, of moulding
the rim slightly out-turned, and thickening its metal.
Here at last we should have a real bell with the
so-called sound-bow, or thick lip. It is, however,
generally supposed that Europe was the birth-
place of modern bells; they seem not to have
existed as musical instruments until the Middle
Ages. Of the bells of the Bible, therefore, we
have but little to say. They were mere
accoutrements, not capable of being arranged
so as to produce the consecutive sounds of a
musical scale. The care bestowed upon their
form and construction, particularly in Holland
and Belgium, led to the casting of those rich
and mellow-toned instruments whose sounds
ever stir deep emotions in us, whether of joy or
sorrow. England was not slow to adopt so appropriate and useful an addition to her many church
towers, and learned to make use of them in a way
even now imperfectly understood on the Continent
—namely, that of hanging them on the axis of
a wheel, and ringing them by a complete swing.
The most ancient bells yet discovered are found
not to be castings, but to consist of a plate of
metal, bent round, and rudely riveted where the
edges meet. Bells, then, are closely allied to
cymbals, but when mentioned in ancient authors

are not to be looked upon as musical instruments. The Assyrians used them, as did the ancient Chinese, and not a few have been found in Irish bogs, or in the drift. If, then, the "bells on horses" were not little cymbals, they were not more than toy-bells, such as were often to be heard in our own country lanes, when the miller's team was lazily led along under the autumn sun, warning any wagoner coming in an opposite direction to draw near the hedge and allow a free passage. *Pha-amon* or *Phaghamon* is the name used in Exod. xxviii. 33-35, for such bells on the priests' garments: "And beneath upon the hem of it thou shalt make pomegranates of blue, and of purple, and of scarlet, round about the hem thereof; and *bells* of gold between them round about; a golden *bell* and a pomegranate, a golden *bell* and a pomegranate, upon the hem of the robe round about. And it shall be upon Aaron to minister: and his sound shall be heard when he goeth in unto the holy place before the Lord, and when he cometh out, that he die not." In Exod. xxxix. 25, 26, we read—"And they made *bells* . . . as the Lord commanded Moses." These are the only two passages in which *pha-amon* occurs.*

Supplementary Notes.

(1.) The reason of the application of the name *cembalo* to the harpsichord and the pianoforte is as follows: In the Middle Ages there was an instrument in popular use consisting of a series of eight or more small bells arranged on a frame and struck with little hammers. It was frequently employed in the music of the Church as an accompaniment to the organ, probably

* See Supplementary Note (3), to this Chapter.

with the idea of emphasizing the plain-chant. The name given to it was *cymbalum* or *cymbal*, for in its earlier stages hemispherical gongs, similar in shape to the ancient hand-cymbals, took the place of bells. When, however, the psaltery, with its wire strings, was struck with hammers, instead of being plucked with the fingers or a plectrum, and so became the dulcimer (as described in Supplementary Note (2) to Chapter iii.), the name of the older bell-chime, *cymbalum*, was transferred to it owing to the similarity of the player's action and the musical tone. The application of keys to the psaltery, which produced the harpsichord, continued to the new instrument the use of the same name, because of the similarity of its clashing tones; while the word *cembalo* as applied to the pianoforte is still more natural, for it is directly descended from the dulcimer.

(2.) The term *nakers*, so frequent in mediæval writings, is derived from the word *nacaire*, or *nakkarah*, the name of a drum used by the Saracens and Arabs. If large, a pair of them are suspended, one on either side of a camel, or, if small, on a man's back, and they are struck with two short sticks. The *nakers* are now represented by our cavalry drums and orchestral timpani.

(3.) The use of bells of large size and musical tone was common in Asia long before they were to be found in Europe. The oldest Chinese bells are not provided with a clapper, but are struck with a hammer on the outside. Little bells of bronze, not hemispherical, but of the recognised bell shape, were frequently attached to the trappings of the Roman chariot horses, and actual specimens have been found at Pompeii.

CHAPTER X.

ONCE only does the word *menaaneim* occur in the Bible—in 2 Sam. vi. 5: "And David and all the house of Israel played before the Lord on all

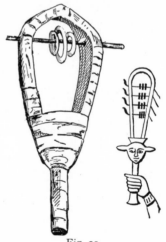

Fig. 90.

manner of instruments made of fir-wood, even on harps, and on psalteries, and on timbrels, and on *menaaneim*, and on cymbals. It is wrongly

translated "cornets"; for the root of the Hebrew word suggests the same as that of the Latin *nuo*, whence *nuto*, "to sway to and fro, to vibrate." *
Now, the word *sistrum* (σεῖστρον) comes from a Greek verb σείω, having an almost identical meaning. There is, therefore, a very good reason for believing that the word *menaaneim* refers to an instrument which vibrated when shaken or rattled. One of the two forms of the *sistrum* answers to

Fig. 91.

this description. Through an upright frame of metal, supported on a handle, several metal rods are passed, and fixed in position, generally by bending their extremities. On them are placed loose metallic rings. Fig. 90 gives an example of this instrument which is preserved in the Berlin Museum. The position of the rings in

* The Revised Version gives "castanets" in the text and "sistra" in the margin. The Septuagint rendering is κυμβάλοις (cymbals), the Vulgate "sistris."—(ED.)

this illustration may perhaps lead to the supposition that they are fixed by the centre; this is not the case. They, of course, should lie loosely on the bars. Fig. 91 shows Egyptian priestesses in the act of playing this kind of *sistrum* at a religious ceremony. The second form of *sistrum*, above mentioned, had metallic bars *without rings*. Hence it has been thought by some that the bars were of graduated length, and gave a series of

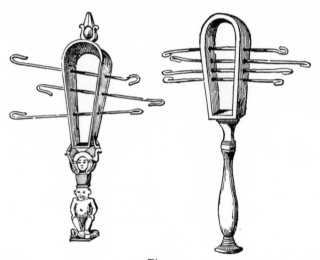

Fig. 92.

musical sounds when struck by some hard substance held in the other hand of the player. Fig. 92 represents two specimens. Their Egyptian name is doubtful, but the word *kem-kem* is thought to apply to them, although the Coptic version translates the "sounding brass" of 1 Cor. xiii. 1 by *kem-kem*. Others think it applies to the tambour. Rosellini has deciphered the word

sescesch, and interprets it as *sistrum*. The Romans
used the instrument, or at least were aware of its
existence, fairly true representations of it being
found on some of their medals. This may
have been the *æreum crepitaculum* of their poets.
As among the Egyptians the *sistrum* often
accompanied rites of a very wanton and lascivious
character, there is something intensely sarcastic in
Virgil's description of Cleopatra leading her forces
to battle to the sound of the *sistrum* :—

" Regina in mediis patrio vocat agmina sistro."

(Virgil, *Æneid*, viii. 696.)

Fig. 93.

The close connection between musical
instruments of apparently very divergent species
has been often before remarked ; it is not surprising,
therefore, to find a link between cymbals and the
sistrum. Fig. 93 shows two such ornamental bars
of metal held one in each hand of the performer ;
and when struck together, they produced a loud

clanging sound to mark the rhythm of a dance. The fact that they were clashed together gives them a relation to cymbals, while their form—that of vibrating rods—renders it difficult to place them otherwise than in the *sistrum* group.*

The word *shalishim* occurs only in 1 Sam. xviii. 6. The *shalish* has been variously described as a triangle, a *sistrum*, and by some—a fiddle! The root implies the numerical value of three: "And it came to pass as they came, when David was returned from the slaughter of the Philistine, that the women came out of all cities of Israel, singing and dancing, to meet King Saul, with tabrets, with joy, and with *shalishim*" (margin, "three-stringed instruments"). Whatever may be the antiquity of the viol family, it is difficult to believe that an instrument which must have been in very common use—as the people flocked together who could play it "from all cities of Israel"—should only incidentally be mentioned once in the whole course of Jewish chronicle. The notion that all the women of Israel were experts on a three-stringed fiddle is certainly novel, and, to say the least, very absurd. A triangle it might have been, but it is more probable that it was a *sistrum*, either with three rings on each bar, as in Fig. 90, or with three vibrating bars, as in Fig. 92.†

Fortunately there is but little doubt as to the nature of the *toph*. It was a tambour, timbrel, or hand-drum. All nations seem to have possessed drums of various kinds, but always of a comparatively small size. It remained for

---

* These instruments were made of split wood, and were used as rattles like the Greek and Roman *crotala*.—(ED.)

† See Supplementary Note (1), to this Chapter.

modern Europeans to produce the gigantic
specimens which are now to be found in our
orchestras. Such drums were never dreamt of by
the Ancients. The necessity for having portable
instruments would have precluded their use, even
if their presence had been thought desirable.
Modern tambours, or tambourines, as we more
usually term them, are invariably round in shape;
those of the Ancients, especially of the Egyptians,
were sometimes oblong or square. Fig. 94 exhibits
both kinds in use. They were among the chief

Fig. 94.

embellishments of their funeral lamentations, which
seem to have been of a prolonged character. It
is said that such ceremonies, when a prince died,
lasted as many as seventy days. Then they sang,
or uttered their mournful cries, to a tambour
accompaniment. But the Egyptians also had
drums of two other kinds. One consisted of a
wood or copper cylinder covered at both ends with
parchment, the two heads being beaten with the
hands, just as the tom-tom of India is played.
The Egyptian " long-drum," as it may be called,

was, both as to size and shape, very similar to this tom-tom, which is not infrequently to be seen in the hands of some poor wanderer from our distant empire, who is begging upon the streets of London. Fig. 95 shows the manner in which it was carried

Fig. 95.

Fig. 96.

and beaten. The other instrument of this class is peculiarly interesting, as being evidently the prototype of our modern kettledrum. It is called *darabooka*, and is formed by stretching parchment over the open end of a basin of metal or earthenware.   When, as was the case in ancient times, this drum or " tabret " was small and easily carried, the termination of the hollow bowl by a handle was ingenious and useful.   But as the size increased, the handle had to give place to three feet, and the metal bowl could be rounded— a form greatly to the advantage of free vibration. Our kettledrum is therefore little else than a very large *darabooka*, standing on a tripod, instead of terminating with a handle.   The *darabooka* is shown in Fig. 96.

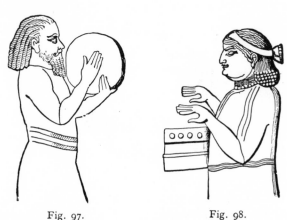

Fig. 97.   Fig. 98.

The Assyrians appear to have used the tambour, and also a drum suspended by a cord round the neck (see Figs. 97 and 98).   But the instrument they thus carried seems not to have been beaten, like the Egyptian long-drum and the Indian tom-tom, at both ends, but only at its upper surface.

Two questions arise with regard to ancient drums and tambours : Was the parchment or head of the drum rigidly fixed, or was it capable of being tuned ? The reader is no doubt well aware that to the edges of the heads of a modern drum is attached, in the bass drum and side-drum, a series of cords, and in the kettledrum a metal ring, by means of which the parchment can be tightened or loosened, and consequently a power of regulating the pitch is obtained. Probably the head was fixed, and the ancient drums and tambours could not be tuned.* The lines which cross the long-drum of the Egyptians in Fig. 95 look very much like the cords which pass over the sides of our side-drums,

Fig. 99.

but these cross-bars are evidently only a rude attempt at ornamentation. The second question is, Had the ancient tambours little bells, plates of metal, or castanets inserted in the rim, as we have in our tambourines ? Probably they had. Fig. 99 shows an Arabian tambour called *bendyr*. There are holes in the rim of this which unmistakably suggest the probable insertion of some such a kind of pulsatile contrivance. Moreover, it is known that such appendages were not strange to the Greeks. The *bendyr* also contains five strings

* See.,however, Supplementary Note (1), to this Chapter.

stretched across the inner surface of the head, as
seen in the illustration, for the purpose of reinforcing
its tone. Such a construction seems to have been
introduced in comparatively late times. Stretched
strings were formerly used for a like purpose in
instruments of several other kinds, notably in the
stringed instrument called *viola d'amore*, in which
metal strings were stretched under those of catgut,

Fig. 100.

passing under the finger-board and through the
middle of the bridge, which was pierced to receive
them. The Arabs have three varieties of tambour
besides that called *bendyr*. One of them, the
mazhar, smaller than the *bendyr*, has no rever-
berating strings, and has metal rings instead of
castanets. Another, the *târ*, has, like the *mazhar*,

no stretched strings, but has four copper castanets. The fourth kind has only two castanets. Goatskin generally forms the head of these Arabian tambours, which are chiefly played by women, as was the case among the ancient Egyptians. The Arabians have drums, not unlike kettledrums, and they may be seen playing them on horseback or camelback just as the kettledrums are carried and played by the bands of our cavalry regiments. Fig. 100 (p. 187) shows a fine specimen of an old tambour in the Kensington Museum collection, which has not only castanets in the rim, but bells suspended in the interior.

It is impossible to say whether the Hebrews used the drum as well as the tambour (timbrel): probably the word *toph* represented only the latter. Its antiquity is proved by the fact that mention is made of it in conjunction with the *kinnor*, in the passage once before quoted (Gen. xxxi. 27), where Laban rebukes Jacob for having left him stealthily, whereas an honourable departure would have been accompanied with songs, *toph*, and *kinnor*.

It was a *toph* which Miriam took in her hand when she led the song and dance on that wondrous day when Israel saw the "great work" which God had done, and thankfulness burst forth from side to side as they answered one another: "Sing unto the Lord, for he hath triumphed gloriously" (Exod. xv. 1). Very different were the feelings which filled the breast of Jephthah when his only child came forth with *toph* in hand to welcome his victorious return from unequal fight with Ammon.

Among the instruments which the prophets were carrying when the future King Saul met them, was a *toph* (1 Sam. x. 5), and the same instrument was

ere long to be a source of jealousy and chagrin to
him when the women of Israel praised the youthful
hero David on his return from slaying the giant;
and it was part of the music which graced the
return of the Ark from Kirjath-jearim.   That the
use of the timbrel was not limited to religious
ceremonies is plain from the allusion in Isaiah v. 12.
It seems not to have been carried in warfare.   On
the contrary, in the following passage from Isaiah
(xxx. 32) its mention is apparently intended to
show the cheerful peace which everywhere should
follow on the smiting of the Assyrian—" And in
every place where the grounded staff shall pass,
which the Lord shall lay upon him, it shall be
with *tabrets* and harps."   The tambour has now been
excluded from sacred buildings, having given place
to the more solemn and imposing drum.

It may perhaps be said that in speaking of the
probable nature of the *kinnor* and *nebel,* too much
reliance has been placed on the argument that
people have a tendency to use light portable
instruments when travelling, and larger instruments
in religious and civil ceremonies.

If, however, we consider the habits of the present
day in this respect, we shall find more support of
the argument than might at first be supposed.
For example, street-singers who travel from place
to place over long distances, have more or less
adopted the portable *banjo* as an accompaniment
to the voice, leaving the full-sized guitar and the
large harp either to the concert-room or to street-
musicians who remain in large cities.   Then, again,
although the two once well-defined classes of
portative and *positive* organs have merged or died
out, there still remains the *positive* organ in our

churches and halls, and the *portative* barrel-organ whose existence can still be verified by the sad experience of all lovers of quiet.

As regards drums, we certainly possess the light tambourine, and the large kettledrums of concert use. The portable violin, called *kit* in England, has now become obsolete, but its French name *pochette* fully points out the fact that its popularity was owing to its convenience as a *pocket-fiddle*. The same remark may be applied to the pianoforte, for although large instruments mechanically played are now wheeled about our great cities, there was formerly a marked distinction between the portative pianoforte played by gipsy women and the heavy instrument placed in drawing-rooms.

It would seem justifiable, therefore, to assume that nomadic tribes would use small, simple types of instruments, while the inhabitants of great cities would also use instruments of more elaborate construction and of greater capabilities in their worship or court-ceremonies.

Supplementary Notes.

(1.) On the word *shalish*, as meaning a three-stringed instrument (probably the long-necked guitar or *tanboura*), see Supplementary Note (2), to Chapter ii. The association of the tambour with stringed instruments was very general, and found with the *kinnor* and *nebel*. In the same way, we still have in negro minstrelsy the association of banjo and tambourine. There is at present no proof of the use of the triangle by ancient Eastern peoples, though the word *shalish* has been supposed to denote this instrument.

(2.) The use of the hand-drum at wedding festivities is alluded to in the First Book of the Maccabees (ix. 39): "And the bridegroom came forth and his friends and brethren to meet them with drums (*tympana*) and instruments of musick and many weapons."

As regards the employment of "bracing" cords for tightening the skin heads of the drum, the Egyptians at any rate were well acquainted with them, for they were still attached to an ancient instrument found at Thebes in 1823. They also used the "snares" which give to our own side-drum its peculiar tone; these strings, however, are not for sympathetic purposes, as Dr. Stainer suggests, but are intended to rest on the parchment head and thus to increase the rattle or "snap" when the drum is struck. A Note on the Oriental kettledrums, or *nakers*, has been already appended to the preceding chapter.

PART IV.

VOCAL MUSIC OF THE HEBREWS.

CHAPTER XI.

THE absence of monumental records of Hebrew music, some of which, however, may yet be found by the zealous explorers now at work in Palestine, renders the subject of the vocal music of the Jews no less involved in difficulty and mystery than that of their musical instruments. And in offering a few remarks upon it, the course already pursued seems to be the only one open to us—namely, to attempt to give some general idea of what ancient vocal music was, and leave it to the reader to judge how far the Hebrews caught the artistic spirit of their age, or were led by an unusual share of musical ability to excel their neighbours or contemporaries in the practice of this art. If a set of pipes could be found, in good preservation, in each of the centres of ancient civilisation, an approximation might be made to the *scales* commonly in use; but, alas! when the treasures of European museums are ransacked, and some of the envied specimens produced, it is found that they are too old and crumbling to bear handling, or, if they may be freely handled, resolutely decline to emit a sound of any kind. Facsimiles, it is true, can be constructed. But, as has been hinted in a previous chapter, the method of blowing into a reed-pipe, or of closing or half-closing the apertures, has all to do with the reproduction of its scale ; so that even if an ancient pipe were actually placed in the hands of one of our most expert players, he could only give us a general idea of its original capabilities. From ancient instruments of the harp or guitar class which have survived still less information can be gleaned. It is hardly necessary to say that, at the most, only fragments of the strings remain attached to their frames ; nor would an intact set tell any tale, as stringed instruments are not in the habit of remaining in tune for several thousands of years.

Of course *written* music, or the use of signs to represent sounds, must have been, in point of time, far posterior to the use of both vocal and instrumental music. Even if music had never had a definite scientific growth, it could not have failed to creep into use from a common observance of the different effects produced by altering the pitch of the voice, especially when reading poetry. Whilst reciting the great deeds of ancestors, or traditional hymns on the greatness of the unseen Maker of the universe, the modulation of the voice must have been a most important element of the poet's or minstrel's training. Bearing this fact in mind, it is easy to imagine how, first of all, a solemn monotone, next, occasional changes of pitch, and, lastly, ornaments and graces, came to be part of

the reciter's art, or, in other words, the poet's *music*.
The Arabs to this day recite the Koran to a sort
of irregular chant or cantillation. Among many
nations musical instruments were used to support
the voice of the chanter. That the prophets of
Israel sometimes uttered their inspirations in such
a manner is suggested in 1 Sam. x. 5. It is a well-
known fact that ancient Greek poets rhapsodised
in a sing-song way often to the accompaniment of
a lyre or pipe.* The traditions of such accompaniment were probably handed down to the Italian
improvisatori, and the troubadours, whose rhymes
were frequently sung to chant-like melodies.

How to write these modulations of the voice was
quite another question. And here we find that
ancient musical notation seems naturally to have
grown into two branches, the difference between
them depending upon the taste or aptitude of
different nations for incorporating into their music
sounds of fixed pitch, or ornaments and graces
which could be used in any pitch according to the
reciter's wish or requirements. At once the fact
suggests itself to us that flutes or wind instruments
would have a tendency to fix definite pitch, while
harps and guitars, owing to the ease with which
their *accordatura* or system of tuning could be
altered, would be available for a constantly
changing normal pitch,—or *diapason*, as we somewhat improperly term it.

Not forgetting this, it is most interesting to find
that in *notation* the tendency of Europeans has
been from the earliest times to graduate sounds
from a known generator, and so to fix pitch ; while,
on the other hand, the taste for ornament has

* See Donaldson's *Theatre of the Greeks*, notes to p. xiv.

led Asiatic nations to devise means rather for
expressing these ornaments than for securing their
immutability in a scale series.

To this day an Asiatic song generally consists of
a slight melodic framework, almost hidden beneath
a load of extraneous graces.   The following
fragment of an Arabian tune would puzzle the
most devoted lover of *fioritura.*   The notes
marked x are not doubly sharpened, as would
be implied by our modern notation, but express
small intervals lying between the notes of our
scale which we have no means of showing :—

It must not for one moment be supposed that
all Asiatic melodies abound in graces, or that all
ancient European tunes lack them : quite the
contrary.   All that is meant is that the tendency of
these two branches of music is in the one case to
include them, and in the other to exclude them.

Hence we find that the oldest known form of
European notation has for its object the giving of
a sign for a fixed note ; the oldest, or presumably
the oldest, of Eastern systems the giving of a sign
for the *movement* of the voice for a certain interval,
or this same movement with the addition of an

embellishment. The former is exemplified in the Greek notation, as given in ancient treatises; the latter in the so-called accents of the Hebrews, of which more will be said later. Hence, ancient notations are of two kinds : those founded on the use of the letters of the alphabet, and those in which conventional signs described conventional ornaments. These two, however, though distinct in principle, often overlap each other. The ancient notation of the Eastern Church, which was tabulated by St. John of Damascus, who was to the Eastern Church, musically, what Gregory was to the Western, consisted of signs which must be considered as indications of the *form* of the movement of the music-director's hand. Much can be said in favour of this theory, as a system of *chironomy* has been associated with music from the earliest times.*   A few are here given :—

⌒	. . . . . Ison. *tonic*
—	. . . . . Oligon.
╱	. . . . . Oxeia.
ᴜ	. . . . . Pentasthe.
⌂	. . . . . Kouphisma.
Ч	. . . . . Pelasthon.

* See *Anthologia Græca Carminum Christianorum*, Christ et Paranikas. In the modern Tonic Sol-fa system the use of hand-signs is retained.

Ison is the keynote or tonic, a movable *Doh*. The other signs represent the vocalisation of various intervals above ; namely, the second, third, fourth, fifth, and sixth.

If such distinctive signs as these were used only for the expression of definite intervals, the translation of such music into modern notes would be comparatively easy ; but unfortunately the Hebrew accents were intended in all probability to describe often not only an interval, but a succession of notes and an embellishment. The reading of the sacred Scriptures, says De Sola, was " always accompanied by the observance of certain signs or accents, intended to determine the sense, and as musical notes; which, although they have a distinct form or figure, do not, nevertheless, present a determinate sound like our present musical notes, but their sound is dependent on oral instruction, since the same sounds vary in sound in the various scriptural books, and are modulated according to the tenor and contents of them." De Sola then goes on to quote R. Simeon bar Zemach Duran, to the effect that of the accents, which are sorts of melodies, three have remained : one appropriated to the reading of the Pentateuch; the second for that of the Prophets (the portion used on Sabbaths and festivals differing from the rest) ; the third for the reading of the Psalms, the Proverbs, and Book of Job.*   Some of these signs are placed over words, others under; some over the last letter of a word, last but one, or in other

---

* The Sephardim have also melodies for the Books of Esther, Ruth, Song of Solomon, and Lamentations of Jeremiah. Not only the canonical books of Scripture, but the Mishna and probably the Jemarah, were recited to cantillation; an edition of the Mishna as late as 1553 was printed with musical accents. (De Sola, p. 12.)

positions, the musical value varying accordingly. The following is a list of them as given by Fétis :—

↘	Paschta.	✓	Kadma.
L	Munahh.	♈	Thélisha ghédola.
∿	Zarka.	♇	Karné pharah.
⦂	Ségoal.	⌐	Phazer, or Pazer Katon.
ᔓ	Schalscheleth.	ᴠ	Zakef Katon.
♀	Thalsha.	ᴒ	Zakef ghadol.
ᔕ	Dargha.	⸵	Rabia.
ᘉ	Thebhir.	Ͻ	Athnahh.
ᘁ	Aslà.	ᴗ	Soph pasouk.
ᴖ	Ghéresh.	⌐	Légormi.
≊	Schené Gherischaim.	⟨	Jérach Ben iomo.
U	Mercha.	ᛙ	Maphach.
ᴧ	Jethib.		

The form of several of the above will be found to differ from that given to them in other works, because in the manuscripts from which the accents are copied, it has varied slightly from time to time.* Kircher (*Musurgia*, 1650) exhibits their position above or below a word by using a short line as an imaginary word. Some of the vowel-accents of Hebrew become tonal-accents if placed in a particular place with regard to the letters forming

---

* The titles given to the accents in the above extract from Fétis (*Histoire Générale de la Musique*) are in their French form : the commonly accepted English transliteration of the Hebrew names will be found in Appendix IV.—(ED.)

the word. This adds to the difficulties of this already difficult subject. The following, in modern notation, are some of Kircher's explanations of the accents* :—

Schalscheleth   (or)

Pazer Katon.   Zarka.

Dargha.

A careful examination of Kircher's complete list will, however, raise some doubts as to his trustworthiness. Exactly similar musical phrases are in more than one instance given for two different accents, and the explanation of some of them resolves itself into the repetition of a single note.

The questions which arise as to the meaning of these signs would pass from the consideration of the musician to that of the scholar, were it not for the fact that complete musical transcriptions of them, such as those above, have been given by several authors. On comparing these, however, their difference is found to be so great that the conclusion is unwillingly forced upon us that practically the musical rendering of the accents varies in character according to the nature of

* In the original edition these examples were wrongly transcribed: Dr. Stainer apparently did not observe that Kircher arranged the explanations of the accents to read from right to left, *i.e.*, the same way as the Hebrew words which accompany them.—(ED.)

music in use in whatever country the Jews have become domiciled. Thus Eastern Jews give them in music which bears a close likeness to that of modern Asiatics. Their interpretation in Spain is palpably Moorish; in Germany it is different from both of these, and so on. The few following examples will point out the discrepancies which exist in their explanation.

Schalscheleth, which has already been quoted from Kircher, is traditionally rendered in the Egyptian synagogues :—

by the English Jews, according to Nathan (*Essay on History of Music*) :—

by the Spanish Jews, according to Bartolocci (*Bibliotheca Magna Rabbinica*) :—

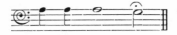

Any translations more divergent in character than these can scarcely be conceived. In comparing traditional tunes it is generally, or at least often, found that the different versions begin and end in the same key-tonality; but in comparing the above four traditional explanations of *schalscheleth* not even this similarity of construction is observable.

It should be remarked that the musical renderings of the accents, as given by Egyptian and Syrian Jews, bear a striking resemblance to each other. For instance, *thalsha* is thus sung by the Egyptian Jews (according to Fétis) :—

The Syrian use is practically identical :—

It has also been found that two sects of Jews in Egypt, though opposed to each other in ceremonial and doctrine, have very similar systems of singing the accents.

As the primary use of accents is to point out the usual elevation of the voice—as shown by the Greek accents, which were a comparatively late addition to their written language, for the benefit of foreign students—so also it is quite possible that these complicated Hebrew accents gradually grew out of what were originally simple signs directing a slight elevation of the voice when reading or perhaps monotoning. That monotone, when used from century to century in the mouth of devout readers, would grow into a cantillation, or rude sort of chant, can be proved by the history of our early Church plain-song. Why should not the Hebrews in their day have passed through the same phases of musical development as have other nations ?

If there is any truth in this thought it would be futile to attempt to stereotype, as it were, the actual meanings of their tonal accents. In the most primitive times, what would now strike us as a simple cadence of the voice must have added dignity to the solemn recitation of the revered words of the treasured rolls. As art evolved, these improvised ornaments would naturally become more complicated, until, as we actually find to be the case, they would rival the most ambitious modern *roulade*. In the authors already quoted, the reader who is specially interested in this subject will find much information.* A quotation (from Naumbourg) of a fragment of Genesis xxii. shows the result of strictly applying the meaning of the accents attached to the text of the Pentateuch, as interpreted or taken down from tradition by him :—

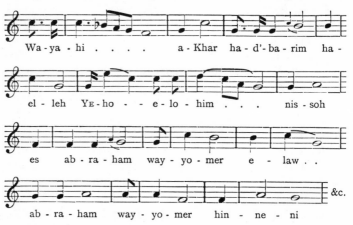

The final close of the passage of which the above is part is on the note F.

* See Supplementary Note (1), to this Chapter.

It is curious that one of the earliest attempts at musical notation among Western Christians should have consisted of signs, such as the following, placed over words :—

The above, which comes from a work of the 11th century, has been copied from Coussemaker's admirable *History of Harmony in the Middle Ages.** As a class these signs were called *neumes*, but sometimes also *accents*. They laboured under precisely the same disadvantages as their prototypes among the Hebrews, namely, the probability of a diversity of translation. Modern musicians perhaps do not know how grateful they ought to be to those who first used *lines*, or a *staff* of lines, to represent the exact interval between ascending and descending sounds. Attempts were probably made to introduce them at about the same date ascribed to the above signs, after which their use rapidly spread. Until such a system came into existence music was chained within the narrowest limits. By enabling composers to express in a simple form the relation or position of two or more parts placed over one another, it doubtless paved the way for that

* *Histoire de l'Harmonie au Moyen Âge*, par E. de Coussemaker (Paris, 1852). See also *The Story of Notation*, by C. F. Abdy Williams (London, 1903).

marvellous expansion of harmony, or polyphony, into a separate branch of the art, which has achieved such wonders in our own day. For although early composers of part-music, it is presumed in accordance with fashion, rarely published scores of their works, it cannot be doubted that in the quietude of their study they took the simple course of sketching a score before copying out separate parts. This growth of harmony must be looked upon as the distinctive feature of modern music. By "harmony" must of course be understood that independence of movement in the component parts of music which makes some of our finest music practically into a number of beautiful melodies heard simultaneously. This, it is almost a certainty, was unknown to all ancient nations. In the more limited sense of the word—"a combination of consonant, or properly regulated dissonant, sounds," or, in short, chords—the Ancients no doubt may be said to have had harmony, that is to say, certain notes of their scales were very probably accompanied by chords, according to certain rules. Yet they had only one melody at a time, whereas we can, and do, listen to many conjointly. And who can describe the pleasure which accrues to a trained musician when he grasps in his mind many threads of delicious melody, and traces the composer's genius in interlacing them, now drawing them close together, now spreading them out until the ear is taxed to gather in high and deep tones; and still further, while thus interweaving the several threads, is spreading to the ear at each combination, whether the parts move concordantly or are discordantly jostling one another, chords which are in themselves

complete and beautiful sets of sweet sounds?
Such harmony—to be found in the works of a
Bach, Handel, Mozart, Beethoven, or Mendelssohn
—did not exist for the Hebrews, Egyptians, or
even Greeks. It places modern music on a
pinnacle of glory. Chords, and a regulated use
of chords, the Hebrews very probably used; but
they did not possess the full gift which we
term harmony.

As regards the form of early Hebrew melodies,
it is probable that they are reflected in modern
Asiatic music, and would, if we could hear them
now, strike us as being in a sort of minor mode.
It is possible that they might at one time have had
an enharmonic scale (that is, a scale having intervals
less than a semitone), and that this was in time
superseded by a simpler form ; but there are good
reasons for supposing that they used a form of
scale consisting of tones and semitones. From
some of the music now sung by Egyptian Jews
such scales as the following might be formed :—

In all attempts to construct scales from
traditional songs, the great difficulty which

presents itself is to discover what was the key-note or starting-point of the scale. If ancient melodies began or ended on the key-note or tonic, the knot could at once be unravelled; but this no one can venture to assume. The key-note of the Greeks was at first, unquestionably, in the middle of their scale. The reader must bear in mind that the question is not of what sounds any tune is made up, but in what order did these sounds occur to form a scale. Engel has shown his appreciation of this difficulty when discussing the *pentatonic* scale, to which he justly attributes great antiquity.* It consists of what we should call the first, second, fourth, fifth, and sixth degrees of our modern scale, *e.g. :—*

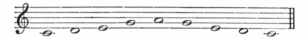

In some of the oldest known tunes made up of these notes, the lowest note is not the tonic. But if it be written thus:—

it presents a very different appearance to the eye, and produces a very different effect on the ear. Yet, without doubt, any musical instrument tuned to a series of notes corresponding to the above might with justice be described as possessing a pentatonic scale. Some interesting remarks on

* See Supplementary Note (2), to this Chapter.

the almost universal use of this pentatonic, or
pentaphonic, scale will be found in Gevaert.*

The following beautiful tune is Syrian. Simple
harmonies have been added to it for the assistance
of those who cannot harmonize it for themselves:—

The rhythm of this tune is so symmetrical that
it might well be used as a hymn-tune. In this
respect it is perhaps different from many of its class.
It will be noticed that its compass is a minor sixth,
a compass within which old melodies are often
contained, and which had been remarked by
Villoteau as a feature in some of the Egyptian-
Jewish music.

The following melody was sent to M. Fétis,
whose account of the vocal music of the Jews is
perhaps the most interesting and reliable portion
of his *Histoire Générale de la Musique* (and to whom
we are indebted for much of the music that has

* *Histoire et Théorie de la Musique de l'Antiquité;* Ghent, 1875.

been given), by a resident of Egypt, as being traditional in the synagogue of Alexandria :—

The quaint and wild beauty of this tune will be appreciated by the most unmusical reader. As an example of ancient Hebrew music, the tune which follows is given with a simple pianoforte accompaniment. It is called the "Song of Moses." De Sola says that a very ancient Spanish work affirms that it was the veritable melody sung by Miriam and her companions. Such a legend goes to prove that the melody probably belongs to a period anterior to the regular settlement of the Jews in Spain :—

Here, in the lone waste, Her song let Israel raise, Un-to

God in the cloud of glo - ry, That guideth her al - way; A - do -
- nai, A-bra-ham's God, A - do - nai . . we praise, For Thy
an - gel ev- er is near, In the cloud to shield by day, In the

fire by night   to   cheer,   Pointing still our homeward way.

VERSES 2 & 3 (*to same accompaniment*).

2. Still,   still wand'ring   on,   A . . trust - ing, timorous
3. Sing   high to   the   Lord   The   strains that Mo - ses

band, Fed with the man   —   na from Hea - ven, We
sang, When Mi - riam took . . up the sto - ry, With

seek our Father's land, A- do - nai, mighty in   war, Hold us
tuneful timbrel's clang. "A- do - nai, ho - ly and strong," Was the

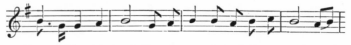

in   Thy right hand, There is none, O Lord, like to Thee, That
shout from hosts that rang, For Thine arm mighty is, O Lord, Who

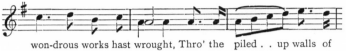

won-drous works hast wrought, Thro' the   piled . . up walls of
tri - umphs glo - rious-ly,   Scat- t'ring our   foes . . . . with His

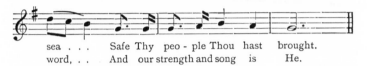

sea . . .   Safe Thy peo - ple Thou hast   brought.
word, . .   And our strength and song   is   He.

In cantillation, which has above been described
as a rude kind of chant, all the defects which are
attached to irregularity and uncertainty showed
themselves. Its character varied from time to
time and in different places. But the very
irregularity of this sort of chant renders it
singularly appropriate for use to poems of a
complicated or constantly changing rhythm, such
as the Psalms. The rigidity of the form of the
single or double chants to which we sing the
beautiful Prayer-book translation of the Psalms is
really their great fault, for although it gives a
congregation of hearers every opportunity of
quickly learning its unvarying tune, yet it must
remain exactly of the same length and cadence,
whether the verses be short or long, or whether the
parallelisms of the poetry run in half-verses, whole
verses, or in sets of two verses. The unequal
length of the mediations and endings of Gregorian
tones has been urged in their behalf, as giving
greater elasticity to the musical recitation of the
Psalms. It must be allowed that this is true, but
on the other hand this advantage is often thrown
away by using one particular tone for a whole
Psalm, or, what is still worse, for several consecutive
Psalms at one service. We moderns, it must be

confessed, stand greatly in need of some easy form
of cantillation for psalm-singing, which, owing to
its elastic character, shall be capable of being
moulded to suit irregularly-constructed poems.
The following chant is used to the 18th Psalm by the
Spanish Jews. As will be seen, it has lost much of
the rhythmical irregularity of cantillation, but yet is
not tied up in a strait-jacket like a modern chant :—

As to the manner in which the Psalms were
rendered at the time of the first Temple, little
can be said with certainty, unless it be that the
instruments we have enumerated were used
in whole or in portions, and that dancing of a
solemn character formed an accompaniment to
the rhythm of the music. Of the psalm-singing
of the second Temple, clearly-defined traditions
are to be found in the Talmud,* according to
which, on a sign being given on cymbals, twelve
Levites, standing upon the broad step of the
stairway leading from the place of the congregation
to the outer court of the priests, playing upon nine
lyres, two harps, and one cymbal, began the
singing of the Psalm, while the officiating priests

* Lange. *Commentary*, Psalms.

poured out the wine offering. Younger Levites
played other instruments, but did not sing; while
the Levitical boys strengthened the treble part by
singing and not playing. The pauses of the Psalm,
or its divisions, were indicated by blasts of trumpets
by priests at the right and left of the cymbalists.*

It will not be difficult to form an opinion of the
general effect of Temple music on solemn occasions
if we know the grand musical results of harps,
trumpets, cymbals, and other simple instruments,
when used in large numbers simultaneously, or in
alternating masses. It is easy to describe it in an
offhand way as barbarous. Barbarous in one sense,
no doubt, it was; so, too, was the frequent gash of
the uplift sacrificial knife in the throat of helpless
victims on reeking altars. Yet the great Jehovah
Himself condescended to consecrate by His visible
Presence ceremonials of such sort, and why may
we not believe that the sacred fire touched the
singers' lips and urged on the cunning fingers of
harpists, when songs of praise, mixing with the
wreathing smoke of incense, found their way to
His throne, the outpourings of true reverence and
holy joy? If one of us could now be transported
into the midst of such a scene, an overpowering
sense of awe and sublimity would be inevitable.
But how much more must the devout Israelites
themselves have been affected, who felt that their
little band—a mere handful in the midst of mighty
heathen nations—was, as it were, the very casket
permitted to hold the revelation of God to man,
of Creator to His creatures; and could sing in the
Psalmist's words, which now stir the heart and
draw forth the song, how from time to time His

* See page 82, under " Selah,' and Note (3), page 90.

mighty hand had strengthened and His loving arm had fenced them !   Let us try and enter into their inmost feelings, when the softest music of their harps wafted the story of His kindness and guidance from side to side of their noble Temple, or a burst of trumpet-sound heralded the recital of His crushing defeat of their enemies, soon again to give place to the chorus leaping from every heart, "Give thanks unto the Lord, His mercy endureth for ever."

When next, in time to come, such sounds wake the desolation of the now ruined and half-buried Holy City, the ancient music will have passed for ever away with the ancient hardness of heart and disbelief, and nothing in Art shall be too new for those who will then understand how old and new dispensations have been bound together in one by Him who has brought His erring children once more unto His fold, from the east and from the west.   What a new, what an unfathomable depth of meaning will then be found in their oft-repeated song, "His mercy endureth for ever!"

SUPPLEMENTARY NOTES.

(1.)   In the suggestive paper by the Rev. F. L. Cohen on the *Ancient Musical Traditions of the Synagogue*, already alluded to in the Supplementary Notes to Chapter iv., the author, when dealing with the music in use at the present time, eliminates from the category of ancient Jewish composition all the choral music now sung with a four-part choir, all music with melodic passages reminiscent of the Gentile musical world, and all tunes set to texts of a measured rhythm, which are at the very earliest the product of mediæval Arab influence.   The oldest vocal traditions of the Synagogue are enshrined in the *Neginoth* —accentual cantillations of Scripture.   In the scrolls used for the public lessons the text is written in consonants alone, and the Precentor has to learn the chant melody by heart : in the printed Bibles, however, the tonic accents for cantillation are added as well as the vowel points.   These accents, some thirty in number, were probably evolved by the Massoretic school of Tiberias about the 7th century A.D. in order to form a notation for the highly developed cantillation which had existed long before, handed down by tradition.   With each individual accent there was associated a particular fixed sequence of notes, and this was sung to the tone syllable of the word as marked by the accent.   These phrases have been preserved with the greatest purity by the Jews of Northern Europe, especially for the reading of the Scriptures and for the chief Prayer. The fixed scales employed are of diatonic and chromatic form (not pentatonic), and even where they are simply diatonic an occasional chromatic change in the embellishment is permitted to the Precentor.   The relation of these scales to the Greek modes has been mentioned in the Notes to Chapter iv.

(2.)   Allusion has previously been made (Chapter iv., Note (2)) to the fact that the musical systems of Assyria and Egypt, so far as can be ascertained, consisted of a seven-note scale : and it is interesting to observe that even where the pentatonic scale is most in evidence at the present day, namely in China and Japan, musicians in both these countries recognise for the classical or ancient music a diatonic scale of seven notes or a chromatic scale of twelve semitones.   In India the ancient scale was divided into twenty-two *sruti* or intervals less than a semitone, and the Persian and Arabian musicians recognise twenty-six of these minute divisions.   There is therefore no reason to believe that the Temple music of the Jews was limited to the much lauded five-note scale.   Encouraged as they were to devote their best to the service of the sanctuary, where masters of music taught and practised their art, it is more than probable that the musical system of the Hebrews was equal, if not superior, to those of their neighbours in Assyria, Phœnicia, and Egypt, where, if we may draw conclusions from the scales still produced by their own flutes and reed-pipes, not only diatonic and chromatic but possibly enharmonic notes were already in favour.

APPENDIX I.—(A).

CLASSIFICATION OF MUSICAL INSTRUMENTS.—1879.

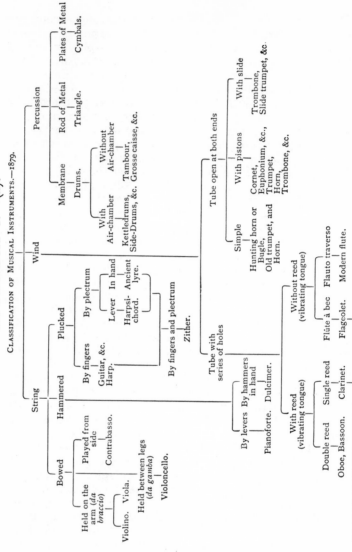

(B).

CLASSIFICATION OF MUSICAL INSTRUMENTS.—1914.

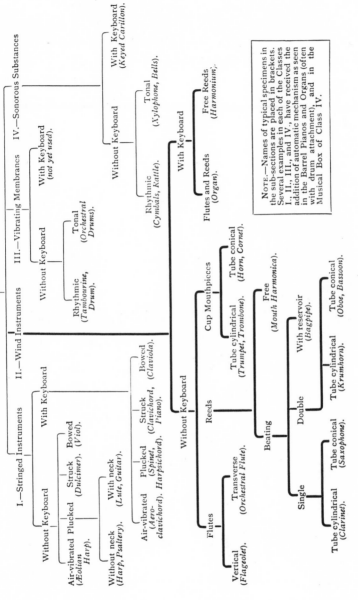

I.—Stringed Instruments

- With Keyboard
  - Struck (Dulcimer). Bowed (Viol).
  - Struck (Clavichord, Piano). Plucked (Spinet, Clavichord. Harpsichord). Bowed (Claviola).
- Without Keyboard
  - Air-vibrated Plucked (Æolian Harp).
  - With neck (Lute, Guitar).
  - Without neck (Harp, Psaltery).
  - Air-vibrated (Aëro-clavichord).

II.—Wind Instruments

- With Keyboard
  - Flutes and Reeds (Organ).
- Without Keyboard
  - Flutes
    - Vertical (Flageolet).
    - Transverse (Orchestral Flute).
  - Reeds
    - Single
      - Tube cylindrical (Clarinet).
      - Tube conical (Saxophone).
    - Beating
      - Double
        - Tube cylindrical (Krumhorn).
        - Tube conical (Oboe, Bassoon).
        - With reservoir (Bagpipe).
      - Free (Mouth Harmonica).
  - Cup Mouthpieces
    - Tube cylindrical (Trumpet, Trombone).
    - Tube conical (Horn, Cornet).

III.—Vibrating Membranes

- With Keyboard (not yet used).
- Without Keyboard
  - Rhythmic (Tambourine, Drum).
  - Tonal (Orchestral Drums).

IV.—Sonorous Substances

- With Keyboard (Keyed Carillon).
- Without Keyboard
  - Rhythmic (Cymbals, Rattle).
  - Tonal (Xylophone, Bells).
- With Keyboard
  - Free Reeds (Harmonium).

NOTE.—Names of typical specimens in the sub-sections are placed in brackets. Several examples in each of the Classes I., II., III., and IV., have received the addition of automatic mechanism as seen in the Barrel Pianos and Organs (often with drum attachment), and in the Musical Box of Class IV.

APPENDIX II

THE HEBREW NAMES OF KNOWN MUSICAL INSTRUMENTS MENTIONED IN THE BIBLE

With the usual Greek and Latin renderings found in the Septuagint and Vulgate Versions.

		Hebrew.	*Greek.*	*Latin.*	*Syriac.*
	KINNŎR	כִּנּוֹר	κινύρα, κιθάρα	cĭthăra	כִּנָּר
	NĒBĔL	נֵבֶל	νάβλα, ψαλτήριον	psalterĭum	
	NĔBĔL ĀSŌR	נֶבֶל עָשׂוֹר	ψαλτήριον δεκάχορδον	"psalterĭum decem chordārum"	
	KHĀLĪL	חָלִיל	αὐλός	tībĭa	
	SHŌPHAR	שׁוֹפָר	σάλπιγξ, κερατίνη	bucĭna, tŭba	
	KHATSŌTSRĀH	חֲצֹצְרָה חֲצוֹצְרָה	σάλπιγξ	tŭba	
	KĔRĔN	קֶרֶן	σάλπιγξ, κέρας	tŭba, cornu	
	UGĀB	עוּגָב	ὄργανον	orgănum	
	TOPH Arab. دُفّ	תֹּף	τύμπανον	tympănum	
	TSĔLTS-LĪM	צֶלְצְלִים	κύμβαλα	cymbăla	
	M'TSIL-TĂYIM	מְצִלְתַּיִם (dual)	κυμβάλω	cymbăla	(Pair of Cymbals.)
	MENAANEIM	מְנַעַנְעִים	κύμβαλα	sistra	(From נוּעַ, *to move to and fro, to oscillate.*)
	SHĀLĪSHIM	שָׁלִישִׁים	κύμβαλα	sistra	
	PHA-AMON	פַּעֲמֹן	κώδων	tintinnābŭlum	
Daniel.	MĂSHRŌKĪTHĀ	מַשְׁרוֹקִיתָא	σῦριγξ	fistŭla	(From שָׁרַק, *to whistle.* See Judges v, 16, where שְׁרִיקוֹת עֲדָרִים = the "pipings" [of those who kept] the flocks.)
Daniel.	KĬTHRŌS	קַתְרוֹס	κιθάρα	cĭthăra	
Daniel.	ŚABECĀ	סַבְּכָא	σαμβύκη	sambūca	
Daniel.	PSĂNTĒRIN	פְּסַנְטֵרִין	ψαλτήριον	psalterĭum	(Called now in Egypt سنطير ; in the Bible وَٱلسَّنْطِير, Dan. iii, 5.)
Daniel.	SUMPONYĀH	סוּמְפֹּנְיָה	συμφωνία	symphonĭa	(Explained by Hebrew interpreters עוּגָב, or "organ.")

APPENDIX III.

THE PRINCIPAL PASSAGES IN WHICH MUSICAL INSTRUMENTS ARE MENTIONED IN THE BIBLE.

Names of which the meanings are not certain are printed in Italics.

TEXT.	INSTRUMENTS MENTIONED.
Gen. iv. 21	Kinnor, Ugab.
Gen. xxxi. 27	Kinnor, Toph.
Exod. xv. 20	Toph (and *Machol*).
Exod. xix. 16, 19; xx. 18	Shophar.
Exod. xxviii. 33, 34; xxxix. 25, 26	Phà-amon.
Lev. xxiii. 24	Keren.
Lev. xxv. 9	Shophar.
Num. x. 2, 8, 9, 10	Khatsotsrah.
Num. xxxi. 6	Khatsotsrah.
Josh. vi. 4, 5, 6, 8, 9, 13	Shophar, Keren.
Judg. iii. 27; vi. 34; vii. 8, 16, 18, 19, 20	Shophar.
Judg. xi. 34	Toph (and *Machol*).
1 Sam. x. 5	Nebel, Toph, Khalil, Kinnor.
1 Sam. xiii. 3	Shophar.
1 Sam. xvi. 16, 23	Kinnor.
1 Sam. xviii. 6	Toph, Shalishim.
2 Sam. ii. 28	Shophar.
2 Sam. vi. 5	Kinnor, Nebel, Toph, Menaaneim, Mtziltayim.
2 Sam. vi. 15; xv. 10; xviii. 16; xx. 1, 22	Shophar.
1 Kings i. 34, 39, 41	Shophar.
1 Kings i. 40	Khalil.
1 Kings x. 12	Kinnor, Nebel.
2 Kings ix. 13	Shophar.
2 Kings xi. 14; xii. 13	Khatsotsrah.
1 Chr. xiii. 8	Kinnor, Nebel, Toph, Mtziltayim, Khatsotsrah.
1 Chr. xv. 16, 19, 20	Nebel, Kinnor, Mtziltayim.

1 Chr. xv. 21, 24, 28	Nebels on Alamoth, Kinnors on the Sheminith, Khatsotsrah, Shophar, Mtziltayim, Nebel, Kinnor.
1 Chr. xvi. 5..	Nebel, Kinnor, Mtziltayim.
1 Chr. xvi. 6..	Khatsotsrah.
1 Chr. xvi. 42	Khatsotsrah, Mtziltayim.
1 Chr. xxv. 1, 3, 5, 6	Kinnor, Nebel, Keren, Mtziltayim.
2 Chr. v. 12, 13	Mtziltayim, Nebel, Kinnor, Khatsotsrah.
2 Chr. vii. 6..	Khatsotsrah.
2 Chr. ix. 11..	Kinnor, Nebel.
2 Chr. xiii. 12, 14	Khatsotsrah.
2 Chr. xv. 14	Shophar, Khatsotsrah.
2 Chr. xx. 28	Nebel, Kinnor, Khatsotsrah.
2 Chr. xxiii. 13	Khatsotsrah.
2 Chr. xxix. 25, 26, 27, 28 ..	Mtziltayim, Nebel, Kinnor, Khatsotsrah.
Ezra iii. 10	Khatsotsrah, Mtziltayim.
Neh. iv. 18, 20	Shophar.
Neh. xii. 27	Mtziltayim, Nebel, Kinnor.
Neh. xii. 35, 41	Khatsotsrah.
Job xxi. 12	Toph, Kinnor, Ugab.
Job xxx. 31	Kinnor, Ugab.
Job xxxix. 24, 25	Shophar.
Psalm v. 1	*Nechiloth.*
Psalm xxx. 11	*Machol.*
Psalm xxxiii. 2	Kinnor, Nebel Azor.
Psalm xliii. 4	Kinnor.
Psalm xlv. 8	Minnim (stringed instruments).
Psalm xlvii. 5 . ..	Shophar.
Psalm xlix. 4	Kinnor.
Psalm liii. (title)	*Machalath.*
Psalm lvii. 8	Nebel, Kinnor.
Psalm lxviii. 25	Kinnor.
Psalm lxxi. 22	Nebel, Kinnor.
Psalm lxxxi. 2	Nebel, Toph, Kinnor.
Psalm lxxxi. 3	Shophar.
Psalm lxxxviii (title)	*Machalath.*
Psalm xcii. 3..	Nebel Azor, Kinnor.
Psalm xcviii. 5, 6	Kinnor, Shophar, Khatsotsrah.
Psalm cviii. 2	Nebel, Kinnor.
Psalm cxxxvii. 2	Kinnor.
Psalm cxliv. 9	Nebel Azor.
Psalm cxlix. 3	*Machol*, Toph, Kinnor.
Psalm cl. 3	Shophar, Nebel, Kinnor.
Psalm cl. 4	Toph (and *Machol*), Minnim, Ugab, Mtziltayim (two kinds).
Isa. v. 12	Kinnor, Nebel, Toph, Khalil.
Isa. xiv. 11	Nebel.
Isa. xvi. 11	Kinnor.
Isa. xviii. 3	Shophar.
Isa. xxiii. 16..	Kinnor.
Isa. xxiv. 8	Toph, Kinnor.
Isa. xxvii. 13..	Shophar.

Isa. xxx. 29 ..	Khalil.
Isa. xxx. 32 ..	Toph, Kinnor.
Isa. lviii. 1 ..	Shophar.
Jer. iv. 5, 19, 21 ; vi. 1, 17	Shophar.
Jer. xxxi. 4, 13	Toph, *Machol.*
Jer. xlii. 14 ..	Shophar.
Jer. xlviii. 36	Khalil.
Jer. li. 27 ..	Shophar.
Lam. v. 15 ..	*Machol.*
Ezek. xxvi 13	Kinnor.
Ezek. xxviii. 13	*Nekeb.*
Ezek xxxiii. 3, 4, 5, 6	Shophar.
Dan. iii. 5, 7, 10, 15	Keren, Mashrokitha, Kithros, Sabeca, Psanterin, Sumphonia.
Hosea v. 8 ..	Khatsotsrah, Shophar.
Hosea viii. 1 .	Shophar.
Joel ii. 1, 15 ..	Shophar.
Amos ii. 2 ; iii. 6	Shophar.
Amos v. 23 ; vi. 5 ..	Nebel.
Zeph. i. 16 ..	Shophar.
Zech. ix. 14 ..	Shophar.
Zech. xiv. 20	*Metzilloth.*
1 Esdras v. 3	Tumpanon, Aulos.
1 Esdras v. 59	Salpinx, Kumbalon.
Judith xvi. 2 ..	Tumpanon, Kumbalon.
Wisdom xix. 18	Psalterion.
Ecclus. xxxix. 15	Kinura.
Ecclus. xl. 21	Aulos, Psalterion.
Ecclus. xlv. 9	Kodon (bell)
Ecclus l. 16 ..	Salpinx (sacred).
1 Macc. iii. 45	Aulos, Kinura.
1 Macc. iv. 40	Salpinx.
1 Macc. iv. 52	Kithara, Kinura, Kumbalon.
1 Macc. v. 31, 33 ..	Salpinx.
1 Macc. vii. 45	Salpinx.
1 Macc. ix. 12, 13 ..	Salpinx.
1 Macc. ix. 39	Tumpanon.
1 Macc. xiii. 51	Kinura, Kumbalon, Nablum.
1 Macc. xvi. 8	Salpinx (sacred).
2 Macc. xv. 25	Salpinx.
Matt. ix. 23 ..	Aulos.
1 Cor. xiii. 1 ..	Kumbalon.
1 Cor. xiv. 7 ..	Aulos, Kithara.
Rev. i. 10 ; iv. 1 ; ix. 14 ..	Salpinx.
Rev. v. 8 ; xiv. 2 ; xv. 2 ..	Kithara.
Rev. xviii. 22	Kithara, Aulos, Salpinx.

APPENDIX IV.

ACCENTS OF THE HEBREW BIBLE.

1. $\left(\overline{}_{|} \right)$ Sĭllūk (end), only at the end of the verse, and always united with $\left(\vdots \right)$ Sōph-pāsūk, which separates each verse.

2. $\left(\overline{}_{\lambda} \right)$ Athnakh divides the verse into two halves, except in Job, The Psalms, and Proverbs.

3. $\left(\underline{\therefore} \right)$ Sĕghōl'tā.‡

4. $\left(\underline{\vdots} \right)$ Zākēph-kātōn.

5. $\left(\underline{\vdots} \right)$ Zākēph-gādhōl.

6. $\left(\underline{\smile} \right)$ Tĭphkhā.

7. $\left(\underline{\cdot} \right)$ Rĕbhīgha.

8. $\left(\underline{\sim} \right)$ Zărkā.‡

9. $\left(\underline{} \right)$ Păshta.‡

10. $\left(\overline{<} \right)$ Yĕthīb.†

11. $\left(\overline{}_{\jmath} \right)$ Thebīr.

12. $\left(\underline{} \right)$ Shălsheleth.

13. $\left(\overline{\smile} \right)$ Tĭphkhā *initiale*.†

14. $\left(\underline{\upsilon} \right)$ Pāzēr.

15. $\left(\underline{\wp} \right)$ Kărnê-phārā.

16. $\left(\underline{\wp} \right)$ Great Tĕlīshā.†

}   DISTINCTIVE ACCENTS.

17. $(\underline{\angle})$ Gărĕsh.

18. $(\underline{\ell})$ *Double* Gărĕsh.

19. $(\;|\;)$ Pĕsīk (*between the words*).

20. $(\overline{\,\mathsf{J}\,})$ Mēr'khā.

21. $(\overline{\,\mathsf{J}\,})$ Mūnākh.

22. $(\overline{\,\mathscr{D}\,})$ *Double* Mēr'khā.

23. $(\overline{\;<\;})$ Măhpăkh.

24. $(\underline{\;\mathsf{J}\;})$ Kădmā.

25. $(\overline{\;\mathsf{s}\;})$ Dărgā.

26. $(\overline{\;\mathsf{v}\;})$ Yārē'kh.

27. $(\underline{\;\mathsf{Q}\;})$ *Little* Tĕlīshā.‡

28. $(\overline{\;\mathsf{L}\;})$ Tĭphchā *final*.

29. $(\underline{\overset{\mathsf{Q}}{\mathsf{J}}})$ Mēr'khā *with* Zărkā.

30. $(\underline{\overset{\mathsf{Q}}{<}})$ Măhpăkh *with* Zărkā.

DISTINCTIVE ACCENTS.·
(*contd.*)

CONJUNCTIVE ACCENTS.

Accents marked † are *prepositive*, *i.e.*, stand only on first letter of a word.

Accents marked ‡ are *postpositive*, *i.e.*, stand only on last letter of a word.

The line in brackets thus (——) is used instead of a Hebrew word, and to show the position of the accents above or below the line.

For fuller information on the accents see—

Driver's *Tenses in Hebrew*, pp. 109-124.

Davidson s *Outlines of Hebrew Accentuation*. (Edinburgh, 1861.)

Gesenius's *Hebrew Grammar*, twenty-first German edition by E. Roediger, Ph.D., and B. Davies, LL.D.

Ewald, *Ausführliches Lehrbuch der Hebräischen Sprache*, §§ 95-100.

APPENDIX V.

THE SHOPHAR IN THE SYNAGOGUE.

As Dr. Stainer has made but passing mention of the use of the *shophar* by the Jews of the present day, the following account is necessary, especially as Rabbinical tradition states that the calls, as still played in the synagogue, are identical with the trumpet flourishes formerly used in the Temple and ordained by the Mosaic law (Num. x. 1-10).

The *shophar* (a word derived from a Hebrew root meaning "bright,' and referring to the brilliant and piercing tone of the instrument) is now generally made out of the horn of a ram. The horn, after having been soaked in hot water and straightened, is left in its natural shape at the larger end (*see* illustrations on page 155), but at the smaller, the top is cut off and the end is pierced. A rudimentary mouthpiece is then formed in the natural horn of the instrument. In the modern synagogue, however, any horn of a clean animal (except that of the cow) may be used. Oriental Jews prefer a twisted horn, often an unstraightened ram's horn: and an example brought from Aden was constructed out of the spiral horn of the African koodoo.

Although the larger or bell end of the *shophar* is now frequently decorated with metal work, no metallic attachment is allowed at the mouthpiece, though the straight ibex-horn, which was used in the Temple, is said to have had a golden mouthpiece. An ancient *shophar* found in Leadenhall Street, London, and believed to date from before the expulsion of the Jews from England in the year 1290, has the shape of the straightened ram's-horn described above.

The sounds produced by a good *shophar*-player are clear and thrilling, the instrument, like the mediæval Cornetts mentioned on page 164, being pressed to the right side of the lips (*see* frontispiece).

The *shophar* is blown in the synagogue on certain special occasions falling between the middle of August and the middle of October, viz., during the month Elul, at the New Year (Feast of Trumpets), at the conclusion of the Day of Atonement, and on the seventh day of the Feast of Tabernacles. In the Temple, according to Josephus (Wars, IV., ix. 12), calls were sounded on the Sabbath at its commencement on Friday evening and at its close.

We find in the Bible various terms referring to the calls, and said to be rightly represented by those now in use. Owing to the short length of the tube but few of the harmonic notes, set out on page 156, can be produced, and even these, because of the faulty bore of the natural horn, are very untrue. Generally only the octave above the fundamental note and the twelfth, or the twelfth and the super-octave, are employed; in fact, the calls do not depend on correct musical intervals, but on definite rhythmic strains. "Any sound is satisfactory," say the Rabbis.

For the first call (*Tekiah*) the player is said to "smite" or produce a clear, distinct note; if the note or notes are prolonged (*mashak*) it is called a "Great Tekiah" (*Tekiah gedoulah*).

For the second call (*Teruah*) the performer is to produce a loud alarm. In the Tabernacle and in the Temple these calls were blown on the long straight trumpet (*khatsotsrah*), and the calls were combined to form flourishes, which ranged in number from seven to sixteen according to the importance of the day; each *Teruah* was to be preceded and followed by a *Tekiah*. After the fall of Jerusalem these calls and flourishes were played in the synagogues on the *shophar*, and, according to the Rev. F. L. Cohen, some doubt arose as to the proper method of performing the *Teruah*. Some played it as a trembling, "crying" note (*yebaboth*), others as three "broken" notes (*shebarim*). About the beginning, therefore, of the 3rd century of our era it was ordered that the flourishes should be played with each of the two methods of rendering the *Teruah*. Hence the calls, as I copied them down from those sounded by the *shophar*-player in the London Western Synagogue, are as follows:—

The holding out of this last note to a great length is considered a special feature in a good *shophar*-player. Engel (*Music of the Most Ancient Nations*, p. 295) has misplaced the titles *Tekiah* and *Teruah* (*shebarim*).

Of three specimens of the *shophar* in my possession one, of white polished horn, is 20½ inches in length; another, of black and white horn, decorated with incised lines, is 14¾ inches; and the third, which I obtained in Jerusalem, is a rough, black, and somewhat twisted horn, 15 inches in length. The measurements are all taken along the outside curve. I am told that the white horns are considered more correct and of greater value than the black specimens.

F. W. GALPIN.

INDEX.

Accents, Hebrew .. 197, 215, 222
——— Explanation of 199, 215
Æreum Crepitaculum .. 181
Aijeleth-shahar .. 80, 89
Alamoth .. 74, 80, 89, 90
Almug 22, 38
Al-taschith 79
Arabian Music .. 195, 214
Ardablis 120
Arghool .. 106, 114, 149
Ascaulos 145
Asiatic Song, Character of 195
Assyrian Cymbals .. 167, 173
——— Drums 185
——— Harp 41, 43, 44, 67
——— Lyres .. 20, 26
——— Pipes.. 56
——— Trumpet 160
Aulos 95, 96, 100, 113, 140
Bagpipes .. .. 145 ff, 151
Balgentreter 128
Banjo 189, 190
Barbiton 27
Bellows 127
Bells on Horses .. 174, 177
——— Robes 176
——— Origin of .. 174, 177
Bell-chimes 68, 176
Bendyr 186
Berbers 22
Berosh 22
Biblical Names of Instru-
     ments 218
——— References to Instru-
     ments 219
Bilig, Blastbelg, Blasebalg 128
Bow 87

Bucina 159
Cantillation .. 194, 201, 211 ff
Capistrum 107
Castanets .. 172, 179, 186 ff
Cembalo .. 64, 68, 171, 176
Chalumeau 96, 146, 157
Chanter of Bagpipe .. 146
Chants for Psalms 211
Cheng 134
Chinese Organs 133
Chironomy 196
Chitarrone 70
Cithara .. .. 26, 69 ff
Citole, Cittern .. 27, 70
Clappers (note) 182
Clarinet 96, 112
Classifications of Instru-
     ments 216, 217
Clavichord 63
Clavicytherium 63
Cornamusa 146
Cornet (modern) .. 157, 164
Cornett (mediæval) 154, 164 ff,
     179, 224
Corno Inglese 97
Crook 161
Crotala (note) 182
Cymbals .. .. 166 ff, 179
——— Bell-chimes 68, 176
Dampers 64
Dancing 109, 111
Darabooka 184
Development of Stringed
     Instruments 27, 43, 84 ff, 94
Dextra, Sinistra, of Pipes 105
Double-pipe .. .. 26, 102 ff
——— of the Lady Maket 105, 114

Double and Single Reeds
96, 112, 114, 151
Doucemelle 68
Drone of Double-pipe .. 105
Drums .. 110, 182 ff, 190
—— Bracing of .. 186, 190
—— Snares of .. 186, 190
Dulciana, ... 54
Dulcimer, Etymology of 53, 68
—— Origin of 54 ff, 67,
170, 176
Egyptian Cymbals 167
—— Drums .. ..183 ff
—— Flutes .. 98, 113
—— Harps 13, 37, 43, 50
—— Lutes .. .. 33 ff
—— Lyres .. 16, 22
—— Pipes 105
—— Rattles 182
—— Sistra 180
—— Trumpet 160
Electrum (note) 22
Fiddlers and Pipers .. 4
Finger-board, Origin of .. 85
Fistula 116
Flauto Traverso .. 98, 113, 115
Flute or Flue-pipe ..95, 96,
113, 120
Flûte à bec 98, 113, 115
Foreign Influences ..vi., 6 ff, 214
Frets 35, 47, 88
Ghuggab .. .. 115 ff, 137
Gingra 96
Gittern 27, 69
Gittith 79, 80, 89
Gongs 170
Greek Influence 53, 89, 90, 150
Greek Lyre 24, 194
Gregorian Chant .. 78, 211
Guitar 25, 27, 33, 35, 45,
69, 94, 193
Gytarah 69
Hackbret 57
Ha-Gittith 70
Halil .. .. .. 95 ff
Hardules 120
Harmonics 156, 224
Harmonium, Origin of .. 136
Harmony, Modern 204
Harp .. 13, 29 ff, 50, 67, 84, 193
Harp Lute 88
Harpsichord 64, 88, 170, 176
Hautboy (see Oboe)

Hebrew Accents 197, 215, 222
—— Explanation of 199, 215
Higgaion 81
Hittite Guitar 94
Horizontal Bellows .. 128
Horn .. .. ..153 ff
Hunting-bow .. 27, 84, 94
Hydraulic Organ 120, 122, 129 ff
—— Reconstructed . 140 ff
Improvisatori 194
Irish Bagpipe 149
Irish Harp, Ancient 26, 31
Ison.. 197
Janissary Music .. 169
Jewish Music, Traditional
7, 208 ff, 214, 224
Jobel 153
Jonath 79, 89
Jubilee 153
Kanoon 61
Katur 70
Kem-kem 180
Keren .. .. 50, 153 ff
Kettle-drum.. 109, 184, 188
Khalil .. .. 95 ff, 101
Khatsotsrah .. .. 157 ff, 225
Kin 57, 68
Kinnor 5, 13 ff, 22, 73, 83,
90, 188
Kintal 169
Kissar 22, 69
Kissari 26
Kit 190
Kitar 69
Kithara (see Cithara) 26, 27,
33, 69 ff
Kithros 69, 73
Koto 59, 68, 94
Kuhreihen 157
Kuitra 69
Leannoth 112
Lute .. 24, 27, 34, 37, 70, 86
Lyres, Ancient 17 ff, 24, 26,
86, 94
—— Position in Playing
18, 24
Lyro-Phœnix 67
Machalath 112
Machol or Mahhol 109
Magoudi 148, 152
Magrepha 120
Mahalath 112
Manghanghim .. ..178 ff

Maschil 112
Mashrokitha, Mishrokitha 50, 139
Mazhar 187
Menaaneim .. .. ..178 ff
Metzilloth 174
Michtam 79
Mikshah 159
Minnim .. 47, 83, 119
Minoan Lute 27
——— Lyre 26
——— Pipe 26
Miriam's Song 208
Modern Hebrew Music 8, 214
Monaulos 140
Moorish Influence .. 8, 200
Mtsiltayim .. .. . 166 ff
Musette 146
Muth-labben .. 79
Nabla 29, 44
Nackers, Nakers .. 172, 177
Nanga 41, 45, 84
Nay 96, 113, 149
Nebel 16, 29 ff, 66, 73, 83, 90
Nebel-Azor 42, 73, 83
Nechiloth 102
Neck 25, 33, 85
Nefer 45, 85
Neginim 75
Neginoth 80, 214
Nehiloth 102
Nekeb 104
Neumes 203
Nose Flute 113
Notation, Greek Church .. 196
Notation, Musical .. ..194 ff
Oaten Pipe 100
Oblique Flutes .. 99, 113
Oboe 53, 96, 101, 112
—— d'Amore 97
—— da Caccia 97
Oliphant 153
Organ, Construction of 123, 144
——— Evolution of 120, 140
——— Use in Church .. 138
Origin of Music 2
Pallet of Organ 125
Pandoura 27, 46
Pan's-pipe .. .. 116 ff, 140
Pentatonic Scale .. 90, 206, 215
Pha-amon or Phaghamon 176
Phagotum 114
Pianoforte 31, 63, 66, 86,
88, 170. 176

Pibau 146
Pibgorn 152
Pifferari 149
Piffero di canna 98
Piob Morh 146
Pipe .. .. 95 ff, 110, 193
Pipe and Dance 109
Pipe and Tabor 110
Pipers 4
Pipes, Egyptian .. 105, 114
——— Keys on .. 95, 113
——— Reeds of .. 100, 112
——— Scales of 114
Pistons of Cornets 157
Piva 146
Plectrum 16, 42, 59
Pochette 190
Poongi 152
Portable Instruments .. 189
Portative Organs .. 122, 189
Positive Organs 122, 123, 189
Prophecy and Music .. 194
Psalmos 24, 137
Psalms, Temple use of
74 ff, 90 ff, 212
——— Titles of .. 74, 79 ff, 89
Psaltery .. 37, 51 ff, 67, 176
Psanterin .. .. 50 ff, 73
——— Etymology of .. 52
Ranz des Vaches 157
Rebab, Rebec .. 86, 94
Reed and Flue Pipes .. 95
Regals 122
Rephaah 110
Resonance-box, Growth of 87
Rhythm in Language .. 3
Roundelay 111
Sabeca .. .. 48 ff, 67, 73
Sackbut 48, 163, 165
Sackpfeife 49, 145
Salpinx 154
Salterio 57, 59
——— Tedesco 68
Sambuca 49, 67, 104
Sampogna .. .. ..145 ff
Sampognatori 149
Santir .. 52, 57, 59, 68
Sarmundal .. . 61, 68
Sautrie, or Sawtry 61
Scales, Ancient 77, 90, 205, 215
Scotch Bagpipe 149
Second Temple, Music of
7. 97, 212, 225

Selah .. .. 82, 90 ff
Sephardic Jews: their Music
8, 197
Serpent 165
Sescesch 181
Shalish 46, 182, 190
Shawm 157
Sheminith .. .. 75 ff, 89
Shiggaion 79
Shophar .. 41, 153 ff, 224
——— Modern use of 156, 224 ff
Shoshannim 79
Shushan 79, 81, 89
Single Reeds 96, 106, 112,
114, 151
Sistrum .. .. 179 ff, 182
Sitar 70
Slider of Organ 126
Slides of Trumpets, &c. 157, 163
Song of Moses 208
Songs of Degrees 79
Sono-koto 59
Souffarah 98
Soung 46
Souqqarah .. 146, 147, 151
Spinet 64
Staff or Stave 203
Streich-Zither 88
Strings, Material of 59, 62, 87
Sumponyah .. .. .. 145 ff
Symphonia .. 33, 50, 145 ff
Syrian music .. 5, 207
Syrinx .. .. .. 116 ff
Tabret 185
Tal 169
Talan 169
Tambour, Tambourine 40, 110,
170, 182 ff, 190
Tambourin à cordes .. 110
Tanboura 46, 71, 190

Târ 187
Tension of Strings 31
Ten-stringed Harp 43
Testudo 2, 94
Theorbo 70, 73
Tibia 95
Tibiæ Utriculares 145
Timbrel .. .. 109, 182 ff
Timpani 177
Tinkling Cymbal 174
Tom-tom 183
Tongue-box 95
Toph .. .. 40, 45, 109, 182 ff
Tourti 147
Transverse Flute .. 98, 113, 115
Triangle 182, 190
Trigon .. .. 13 ff, 49, 67
Trombone 48, 163
Trumpet .. 153 ff, 163, 225
Tsang or Tche .. 59, 68
Tseltslim .. .. .. 166 ff
Tuba 160
Tuba Ductilis 164
Tympanon 68
Ugab .. .. 13, 115 ff, 137
Vertical Flute .. 113, 140
Viol 37, 40, 88
Viola d'amore 187
Viola-Lyra 88
Violin 87, 94
Virginal 64
Water-Organ 120, 122, 129 ff
——— Model of .. .. 140 ff
Yang-kin 57
Zamr 97
Zinken 165
Zither 70, 88
Zitty 148
Zouggarah 146